"MEET ME AT THE LOVELESS"

A SOUTHERN CAFE'S COOKBOOK

"Meet Me at the Loveless"

A Southern Café's Cookbook

compiled by Donna McCabe and Mamie Strowd

COOL SPRINGS PRESS

Cover illustration: Carol Heyer
Cover design: Claudia Williams
Contributing writer: Bob Holladay
Managing editor: Jan Keeling
Recipe editor: Judy Van Dyke
Project production: S. E. Anderson
Proofreader: Ashley Crownover

Meet me at the Loveless: a southern café's cookbook / compiled by
Donna McCabe and Mamie Strowd
p.   cm.
Includes index.
ISBN 1-888608-37-4
1. Cookery, American—Southern style. 2. Loveless (Café)
I. McCabe, Donna, 1931-   . II. Strowd, Mamie, 1931-   .
III. Loveless (Café)
TX715.2.S68M44   1998   98-43872
641.5'09768'434—dc21

First printing 1998
Printed in the United States of America
10 9 8 7 6 5 4 3 2

Cool Springs Press, Inc.
2020 Fieldstone Parkway
Suite 900210
Franklin, TN 37069

*for our mother Ruth Vance Killebrew
and all of our loyal customers*

"Meet Me at the Loveless"

Table of Contents

Recipes

Appetizers

Soups & Salads

Breakfast & Breads

Recipes

Meats

Poultry & Seafood

Recipes

Vegetables & Side Dishes

Desserts

Recipes

Desserts (cont'd.)

HISTORY OF THE LOVELESS I

THERE'S A LOT OF DREAMING that occurs on the American road, whether it be the road east, west, north, or south—or just the road home. The American road runs in our imagination and in our literature as much as in our reality. Poets, novelists, and songwriters have all celebrated that freedom of the road, from Mark Twain, to Walt Whitman, to Jack Kerouac, to Hunter S. Thompson, all the way to William Least Heat Moon and his blue highways, circling in the mind and in the consciousness . . .

Interstates have ruined the American road. Route 66, the National Road (U.S. 40), The Oregon Trail, El Camino Real, and about a dozen others have become parts of our history and legend along with the characters who traveled them: Boone and Crockett, the Harpe Brothers, old Jim Bridger, and the Merry Pranksters, Huck and Tom. The road means freedom, not only from responsibility but freedom from yourself. Why put down roots? There's always another town over another hill.

Americans have always loved their roads and the stops along their roads. The movies have celebrated them—*The Grapes of Wrath, Easy*

Rider, Thelma and Louise—people leaving behind the baggage of their lives and starting again.

The Loveless Motel and Café is a product of the American road, the road that winds from east to west, from Nashville and Centerville toward the Delta all the way to Memphis and the Big Muddy. The Loveless (was there ever a name so wonderfully attuned to the heartbreak and loneliness of the road, or to the country music stars who have helped make it popular?) is a white clapboard structure that could have come out of any number of Hollywood hits: *It Happened One Night* (remember Clark Gable and Claudette Colbert and *The Walls of Jericho*?) to *Psycho* (remember the Bates Motel?) to *Five Easy Pieces* (remember Jack Nicholson and the chicken sandwich?).

Highway 100 out of Nashville cuts through the heart of hill country, through the ridges of Western Davidson and Williamson County, through Hickman County and little towns like Centerville and Pleasantville, Linden and Parsons. At Parsons, near the Tennessee River in Perry County, the highway takes a jog south and picks up again near Decaturville before running almost due west toward Memphis through such communities as Jack's Creek, Deanburg, Toone, and Laconia. Somewhere along the way the official designation changes from Highway 100 to State Route 64, but it doesn't matter—it's still headed west, toward the setting sun.

"I am in love with American names," wrote the poet Stephen Vincent Benet. Imagine a name like Laconia or Pasquo or Fairview. The meaning is in the language—strong, rhythmic, native.

On Highway 100, a few miles north of the Davidson/Williamson County line, sits the community of Pasquo, settled in 1800 by folks from

Virginia and North Carolina who just had to get over the mountains to the new lands of Middle Tennessee. Of course the white settlers weren't here first. That honor belongs to the Cherokee, who described the land between the Big Harpeth and West Harpeth Rivers as "where the current divides or forks." Their name for it was "pask-e-tan-ki." It wasn't a new name. The Cherokee had used it for part of Albemarle County in North Carolina, but somehow it seemed to fit Middle Tennessee, too.

Leave it to the settlers to gum up the name. In 1852, the Nashville and Northwestern Railroad was chartered with plans to extend the line west of Nashville for 168 miles. One year later, with the railroad in mind, a post office was established as Pasquotank (the spelling had already changed). The railroad meant traffic; traffic meant visitors and business and a booming economy. It meant size and incorporation and *being someone.*

There was one problem: the railroad missed Pasquotank in favor of a tract of land three miles to the north. The land was owned by William DeMoss, ancestor of one of the earliest settlers in the area, Andrew DeMoss, whose log home, Belle Vue, was built in 1797 and still stands overlooking the Big Harpeth.

continued on page 24

APPETIZERS

Cheese Balls

Yield: 6 dozen

1 cup butter, softened
2 cups shredded Cheddar cheese
2 cups flour
2 cups crisp rice cereal
Dash of Tabasco sauce
Dash of Worcestershire sauce

Mix the butter and cheese in a medium bowl. Stir in the flour gradually. Add the rice cereal, Tabasco sauce and Worcestershire sauce; mix well. Shape into 1-inch balls. Arrange on a non-stick baking sheet. Bake at 375 degrees for 10 to 15 minutes or until golden brown. Remove to a wire rack to cool.

"People have asked us before to do a cookbook and we just somehow haven't. I don't know why, we just never got around to it until now."
—Donna McCabe

Cheese Straws

Yield: 5 dozen

1 1/2 cups flour
2 cups shredded sharp Cheddar cheese
1/4 cup butter, softened
1/4 teaspoon cayenne pepper
1 teaspoon salt
1 teaspoon baking powder

Combine the flour, cheese, butter, cayenne pepper, salt and baking powder in a food processor container. Process until well blended. Spoon the mixture into a cookie press; pipe onto a nonstick baking sheet. Bake at 350 degrees for 20 minutes or until light brown. Remove to a wire rack to cool. May shape the mixture into balls or roll 1/4 inch thick on a lightly floured surface and cut into bite-size pieces before baking.

A P P E T I Z E R S

Sweet-and-Sour Hot Dogs

Yield: 40 servings

1 jar Gulden's hot mustard
1 jar orange marmalade
1 (10-count) package hot dogs

Heat the hot mustard and marmalade in a small saucepan over medium heat, stirring until blended. Cut the hot dogs into bite-size pieces. Stir the hot dogs into the sauce. Spoon into a serving dish. Serve hot. May substitute cocktail wieners for the hot dogs.

"Most good cooks cook by taste."
—Donna McCabe

Stuffed Mushrooms

Yield: 20 servings

1 pound fresh mushrooms
1 tube crab meat salad

Rinse the mushrooms; remove and discard the stems. Arrange the mushroom caps in a baking pan with the hollow side up. Mound the crab meat salad into each mushroom cap. Bake at 325 degrees for 15 minutes or until bubbly. Transfer to a serving dish. Serve hot. Note: Crab meat salad in a tube can be purchased in the fresh fish department.

Bleu Cheese Dip

Yield: 20 servings

1/3 cup crumbled bleu cheese,
  softened
8 ounces cream cheese, softened
2 tablespoons milk

Cream the cheeses and milk in a small mixer bowl. Spoon into a serving dish. Chill, covered, until serving time. Serve with crackers or fresh vegetables.

Chili Cheese Dip

Yield: 40 servings

1 (15-ounce) can chili with beans
1 medium onion, chopped
3 (or more) jalapeños, chopped
2 cups shredded Cheddar cheese
1 (6-ounce) jar medium salsa

Combine the chili with beans, onion, jalapeños, cheese and salsa in a microwave-safe bowl with a lid; mix well. Microwave, covered, on High for 5 minutes; stir. Microwave, covered, for 5 minutes longer or until the cheese is completely melted. Pour into a dish. Serve hot with tortilla chips or corn chips.

"We're not worried about whether we're going to save a nickel here and a dime there. We always use the best ingredients."
—Donna McCabe

Chili Con Queso

Yield: 50 servings

1 (16-ounce) package Velveeta cheese
1 (10-ounce) can tomatoes with
   green chiles

Cut the Velveeta cheese into large pieces; place in a microwave-safe bowl. Microwave, covered, on High until the cheese melts, stirring frequently. Stir in the tomatoes with green chiles. Pour into a serving dish. Serve with corn chips or tortilla chips.

Curry Dip

Yield: 20 servings

1 cup mayonnaise
1 teaspoon grated onion
1 teaspoon horseradish
1 tablespoon tarragon vinegar
1/4 teaspoon (or more) curry
   powder

Combine the mayonnaise, onion, horseradish, vinegar and curry powder in a small bowl; mix well. Spoon into a serving dish. Chill, covered, until serving time. Serve with fresh vegetables.

"It doesn't matter what the food is. If you're not going to use good ingredients to start with, you're not going to come up with a good product."
—Donna McCabe

Guacamole

Yield: 12 servings

2 avocados, mashed
1 clove of garlic, pressed
2 teaspoons grated onion
Dash of lemon juice
Dash of hot pepper
1/2 cup mayonnaise

Combine the avocados, garlic, onion, lemon juice, hot pepper and mayonnaise in a food processor container. Process until smooth. Spoon into a serving dish. Chill, covered, until serving time. May substitute garlic powder for the fresh garlic.

Vidalia Onion Dip

Yield: 50 servings

2 cups chopped Vidalia onions
2 cups mayonnaise
2 cups shredded Swiss cheese

Combine the onions, mayonnaise and cheese in a bowl; mix well. Spoon into a baking dish. Bake at 300 degrees for 15 to 20 minutes or until the cheese melts. Serve warm with chips.

"At the Loveless, customers get their food right away. This is not a restaurant where you sit for thirty minutes and don't have anything before you to eat."
—Donna McCabe

Roquefort Cheese Ball

Yield: 1 cheese ball

$1/2$ cup margarine, softened
8 ounces cream cheese, softened
1 wedge (or more) Roquefort cheese,
  softened
1 teaspoon Worcestershire sauce
$1/8$ teaspoon grated onion

Combine the margarine, cream cheese, Roquefort cheese and Worcestershire sauce and onion in a mixer bowl until creamy. Chill, covered, until slightly firm. Shape the mixture into a ball or log. Garnish with pecans and parsley leaves. Chill, covered, until serving time. Serve with sliced apples or crackers. Cheese ball may be frozen.

Spinach Dip

Yield: 40 servings

1 (10-ounce) package frozen chopped
  spinach, thawed, drained
1 package Knorr Swiss dry vegetable
  soup mix
2 cups sour cream

Combine the spinach, dry soup mix and sour cream in a bowl; mix well. Spoon into a serving dish. Chill, covered, until serving time.

"Sometimes the Loveless will serve whole fraternities or whole sororities. This past weekend, seventy-five people came in at one time."

—Donna McCabe

Tex Mex

Yield: 20 to 25 servings

1 (9-ounce) can bean dip
1 envelope McCormick's taco
    seasoning mix
1 cup sour cream
2 tablespoons (heaping) mayonnaise
1 medium or 2 small avocados,
    chopped
$^1/_2$ cup (or more) chopped onion
1 cup chopped tomatoes
1 (4-ounce) can sliced black olives

Spread the bean dip evenly in the bottom of a 9x13-inch serving dish. Sprinkle with the taco seasoning mix. Spread a mixture of the sour cream and mayonnaise over the top. Layer the avocados, onion, tomatoes and black olives over sour cream mixture. Serve with tortilla chips.

"People who know country ham understand that its proper curing is at best an inexact science . . . the old-fashioned way of preparing country hams has all but vanished and it is a rare restaurant or market that offers genuine slow-cured country hams for sale. The Loveless gets about as close to that standard as anyone . . ."
—John Egerton, *Southern Food*

If one advances confidently
in the direction of his dreams, and
endeavors to live the life which he
has imagined, he will meet with
a success unexpected in
common hours.

—Henry David Thoreau
Walden

By 1860–1861, the eve of war, the big locomotive engines were passing through Belleview Station (the spelling of that name had changed, too), bending all the prosperity its way. In early 1867, the Pasquotank post office closed; on that same day a new post office was opened in Bellevue near the DeMoss store right by the railroad tracks. So it was Bellevue, not Pasquotank, which became the center of the western Harpeth River area. Soon Pasquotank became just plain Pasquo, looped on one side by the road to Memphis and on the other by a high range of hills called Backbone Ridge. By the early 20th century, Pasquo was just a few homes. Nobody seemed to remember much about that ridge. Gone were those who remembered pioneer days, when another road cut up through the high ground to avoid the swamps and malarial fevers of the Harpeth in spring-flood time, then swung back down into Nashville. Nobody seemed to remember much about the Natchez Trace.

In the midst of the Great Depression, when people were looking for any kind of work they could find, a few enterprising pork-barrelers from Mississippi would remember tales of the old road from Nashville to Natchez, and recall the stories of the pioneers and families and assorted scoundrels who used it. They would see the ladies from the Daughters of the American Revolution holding quiet ceremonies, planting another concrete and steel historical marker, encapsulating another bit of legend into historical certainty.

In the early 1930s, Senator Jeff Busby from Mississippi and his fellow representatives pushed and tugged and cajoled President Franklin Roosevelt into signing two pieces of legislation involving the Natchez Trace. One called for a survey of the "old Indian Trail known as the Natchez Trace" by the Department of the Interior, "with a view to constructing a national road on this route to be known as the Natchez Trace Parkway." The second piece of legislation, which was approved a year or two later, appropriated several million dollars to begin construction of that parkway.

The original Natchez Trace lasted for about thirty years, from 1790 to 1820 and the advent of the steamboat. Suddenly there was a cheaper, easier, and safer way to get back upriver than hiking through the wilds of Mississippi, Alabama, and Tennessee.

Today, after nearly 65 years of construction, the Natchez Trace Parkway is still not absolutely complete, though most of it is. After that first generation of pork-barrelers died off in Mississippi, their confederates in Tennessee picked up the scent, so that it was the northern portion of the road (not a road, really, but a long, narrow National Park—remember that) that got finished first. In the summer of 1996, amid all the hoopla of a presidential campaign, the northern terminus of the Parkway was finished. The terminus crosses above Highway 100, looping around to connect with it right in the heart of that long-abandoned little community of Pasquo.

So maybe the last laugh is on Pasquo, after all. Maybe all those Trace visitors will be getting off on Highway 100, turning east and heading into Nashville for the Ryman, Second Avenue, Garth, and Patty, and all the rest of the Opry stars. If so, then they'll be driving right by that relic of pre-interstate America with its neon sign sticking right up by the road like a Hollywood set: the Loveless Motel and Café.

The name is a misnomer. There is no Loveless Motel anymore. The present owner, Donna McCabe, closed that up years ago, though the white wooden buildings still stretch out back. No, it's the café that brings them in—small, ramshackle looking, with a front porch that leaks a bit when it rains. Nothing fancy about it (though they do keep a menu from the Waldorf Astoria on the wall just to remind folks of what they're not), just good old-fashioned country digs.

continued on page 42

SOUPS
&
SALADS

SOUPS

Artichoke Heart Soup

Yield: 4 servings

2 tablespoons chopped onion

1/4 cup margarine

2 tablespoons flour

1 (10-ounce) can chicken broth

1 1/2 to 2 cups milk

Salt to taste

Red pepper to taste

1 (14-ounce) can artichoke
    hearts, drained

Sauté the onion in the margarine in a medium saucepan until tender. Add the flour and broth; mix well. Cook over medium heat until thickened, stirring constantly. Add the milk. Season with the salt and red pepper. Cut the artichokes into bite-size pieces; add to the soup mixture. Cook until heated through. Ladle into soup bowls.

Gazpacho

Yield: 10 servings

1 (16-ounce) can artichoke hearts

1 (8-ounce) can sliced black olives

1 (28-ounce) can whole tomatoes

1 cucumber, chopped

1 small onion, chopped

1 small green bell pepper, chopped

1 (48-ounce) can vegetable juice
    cocktail

1 teaspoon Worcestershire sauce

1/2 teaspoon lemon juice

Salt and pepper to taste

Drain the artichoke hearts and black olives. Chop the tomatoes, artichoke hearts, black olives, cucumber, onion and green pepper. Pour the vegetable juice cocktail into a large container with a lid. Add the artichoke hearts, olives, tomatoes, cucumber, onion and green pepper; mix well. Stir in the Worcestershire sauce, lemon juice, salt and pepper. Chill, covered, for 24 hours before serving.

"My oldest daughter made some homemade vegetable soup not long ago and she called me up and said, 'Mom, it was almost yours, but there's something missing.' And I can remember so many times I would call Mother up and say the same thing."
—Mamie Strowd

Split Pea Soup

Yield: 6 servings

1 country ham hock

3 quarts water

1 package split peas

1 large onion, chopped

3 ribs celery, chopped

3 carrots, sliced

Salt to taste

Place the ham hock in the water in a large saucepan. Bring to a boil; reduce heat. Cook over medium heat until the ham is semi-tender. Add the split peas, onion, celery and carrots. Season with the salt. Cook over medium heat until the peas are soft and the carrots are tender, stirring frequently. Add water as needed.

"Split pea soup is not available everywhere, you know—I don't know many places where you can go to order it."

—Donna McCabe

Spinach Soup

Yield: 6 servings

1 small onion, chopped

3 tablespoons margarine

2 (10-ounce) cans chicken broth

2 (10-ounce) packages frozen
    chopped spinach, thawed, drained

2 cups milk

3 tablespoons flour

Salt to taste

1 cup sour cream

Grated Parmesan cheese to taste

Sauté the onion in the margarine in a medium saucepan until tender. Add the broth and spinach. Cook over low heat, stirring frequently. Combine the milk and flour in a small saucepan. Cook over low heat until thickened, stirring constantly. Add to the spinach mixture. Season with the salt. Add the sour cream just before serving. Ladle into soup bowls. Sprinkle with the Parmesan cheese.

Bean and Vegetable Salad

Yield: 12 to 14 servings

2 bulbs of garlic
2 (16-ounce) cans French-style
    green beans
1 (16-ounce) can green peas
1 (7-ounce) jar pimento-stuffed green
    olives, drained, sliced
1 bunch green onions, chopped
1 cup slivered almonds
4 ribs celery, finely chopped
4 carrots, coarsely grated
1 cup vegetable oil
1/2 cup vinegar
1 teaspoon Worcestershire sauce
Juice of 1 1/2 lemons or 1 1/2 oranges
3/4 cup confectioners' sugar
1 teaspoon paprika
1 teaspoon dry mustard

Spear the garlic bulbs securely onto wooden picks. Combine the green beans, green peas, olives, green onions, almonds, celery and carrots in a large container with a lid; mix well. Combine the oil, vinegar, Worcestershire sauce, lemon juice, confectioners' sugar, paprika and dry mustard in a bowl; mix well. Add to the bean mixture; mix well. Stir in the garlic bulbs on wooden picks. Chill, covered, for 24 hours. Spoon into a large serving dish; remove and discard the garlic bulbs and wooden picks. May substitute dry purple or Vidalia onions for the green onions. May store in the refrigerator for several days or may be frozen in an airtight container.

"We had a storm, I mean a really bad storm and we'd gotten struck . . . My son and my husband were going around saying something's burning somewhere. Now, the restaurant was packed. They said we've got a fire out there, you're going to have to get these people out, but don't get them excited.

➥

Bleu Cheese Salad

Yield: 6 servings

1 clove of garlic
1/4 cup vegetable oil
1/2 teaspoon vinegar
4 ounces bleu cheese, softened
2 hard-cooked eggs
1 head lettuce

Rub the inside of a wooden salad bowl with the garlic; discard the garlic. Pour the oil and vinegar into the bowl. Mash the bleu cheese and the hard-cooked eggs together in a bowl. Spoon into the oil and vinegar mixture; mix well. Tear the lettuce into bite-size pieces. Toss with the bleu cheese mixture in the wooden bowl just before serving.

Chicken Salad

Yield: 6 to 8 Servings

3 cups chopped cooked chicken
3 ribs celery, chopped
3/4 cup Homemade Mayonnaise
   (page 39)
Grated onion to taste
Pepper to taste

Combine the chicken, celery, mayonnaise, onion and pepper in a bowl; mix well. Chill, covered, to season for 2 to 4 hours before serving.

Well, this man got up and I don't think he missed a bite. He started to leave, but they said the fire was out, and he sat down and started right back again. That fire didn't bother him at all."

—Donna McCabe

Cole Slaw

Yield: 6 to 8 servings

1 head cabbage, shredded
1 carrot, grated
1 cup mayonnaise
1 teaspoon sugar
1/2 teaspoon vinegar
Salt and pepper to taste

Combine the cabbage and carrot in a large bowl; mix well. Add a mixture of the mayonnaise, sugar, vinegar, salt and pepper, tossing to coat. Spoon into a serving bowl. Chill, covered, for 30 minutes or longer before serving.

Shoe Peg Corn Salad

Yield: 8 servings

2 (12-ounce) cans Shoe Peg
    corn, drained
1 cucumber, chopped
1 medium white onion, chopped
2 large tomatoes, chopped
1 tablespoon vinegar
2 tablespoons mayonnaise
1/2 cup sour cream
1/2 teaspoon salt
1/4 teaspoon dry mustard
1 teaspoon celery seed

Combine the corn, cucumber, onion and tomatoes in a large bowl; mix well. Mix the vinegar, mayonnaise, sour cream, salt, dry mustard and celery seed in a small bowl, stirring until blended. Pour over the corn mixture, tossing to coat. Spoon into a serving bowl. Chill, covered, for 4 to 6 hours before serving.

"People just like real food. Now see, this is one thing that makes our place so popular. It is real—just real down-to-earth food."
—Donna McCabe

Cranberry Salad

Yield: 8 servings

1 orange
2 cups cranberries
1¹/₂ cups sugar
1 (3-ounce) package lemon gelatin

Peel the orange; remove the seeds. Process the orange and the cranberries in a food processor until finely chopped. Add the sugar; mix well. Let stand for 1 hour. Dissolve the gelatin in 2 cups warm water in a small bowl. Stir into the cranberry mixture. Pour into a nonstick mold. Chill, covered, until set. Unmold onto a serving plate.

"You can't get more typically Tennessee than that kind of meal."
—Michael Stern, *USA Today,* May 12, 1993

Cranberry and Fruit Salad

Yield: 8 servings

1 quart cranberries, rinsed
2 cups sugar
1 (6-ounce) package lemon gelatin
¹/₂ cup chopped pecans
¹/₂ cup chopped celery
1 cup red grape halves
¹/₂ to 1 cup drained crushed
   pineapple

Combine the cranberries with enough water to cover in a medium saucepan. Bring to a boil; reduce heat. Cook until the cranberry husks burst. Add the sugar; mix well. Cook for 5 minutes over medium heat, stirring constantly. Remove from the heat. Add the gelatin, stirring until dissolved. Stir in the pecans, celery, grape halves and pineapple. Pour into a serving dish. Chill, covered, until set.

Ginger Ale and Grapefruit Salad

Yield: 8 servings

2 tablespoons unflavored gelatin
1/4 cup cold water
1/2 cup boiling water
1/4 cup sugar
1/4 cup lemon juice
1 cup ginger ale
1 (20-ounce) can grapefruit sections
8 maraschino cherries

Soften the gelatin in 1/4 cup cold water in a bowl. Add the boiling water, stirring until the gelatin dissolves. Add the sugar and lemon juice; mix well. Stir in the ginger ale. Add the undrained grapefruit. Pour into a serving bowl. Chill, covered, until set. Arrange the maraschino cherries decoratively over the top before serving.

"We're the Killebrews, that was our maiden name. There were a lot of Killebrews and they were all good cooks."
—Donna McCabe

Potato Salad

Yield: 12 to 15 servings

8 Idaho potatoes
4 to 5 ribs celery, chopped
1/2 green bell pepper, chopped
1 (10-ounce) jar pimento-stuffed
    green olives, sliced
Homemade Mayonnaise (page 39)
Hellman's mayonnaise
1/2 onion
Salt and pepper to taste

Peel the potatoes. Cut into 1-inch cubes. Cook the potatoes in enough water to cover until the potatoes are tender; drain. Let stand until cool. Pour the potatoes into a large bowl. Add the celery, green pepper and olives; mix gently. Add enough of a mixture of both types of mayonnaise just to moisten; mix gently. Grate the onion over the top; stir into the mixture. Season with the salt and pepper. Chill, covered, for 2 to 4 hours before serving.

SALADS

Green Salad with Bacon and Artichokes

Yield: 6 servings

2 hard-cooked eggs
1 (14-ounce) can artichoke hearts, drained
1 head iceberg lettuce
1/4 cup (or more) bleu cheese dressing
4 slices bacon, crisp-fried, crumbled

Chop the hard-cooked eggs. Cut the artichokes into bite-size pieces. Tear the lettuce into bite-size pieces. Toss the chopped eggs, artichokes and lettuce in a large serving bowl. Add enough bleu cheese dressing just to moisten. Sprinkle the bacon over the top. Serve immediately. Excellent served with steak, roast or seafood.

Roquefort Cheese Salad

Yield: 6 servings

1 clove of garlic
1 tablespoon sugar
1 teaspoon salt
Paprika to taste
3 tablespoons vegetable oil
Juice of 1 lemon
1 tablespoon vinegar
2 teaspoons Worcestershire sauce
1 hard-cooked egg
1 cube Roquefort cheese
1 head leaf lettuce

Rub a medium serving bowl with the garlic; discard the garlic. Combine the sugar and salt in the bowl. Sprinkle with the paprika. Add the oil; mix well. Add the lemon juice, vinegar and Worcestershire sauce; mix well. Mash the hard-cooked egg and Roquefort cheese into the mixture; mix well. Tear the lettuce into bite-size pieces. Divide the lettuce evenly into 6 serving bowls. Spoon the Roquefort cheese mixture over the lettuce.

"Mama fed everybody and made everybody feel so welcome, so we grew up that way. We try to do it just the way she did."

—Donna McCabe

Tomato Aspic

Yield: 9 servings

1 (10-ounce) can tomato soup
1 soup can cold water
1 envelope unflavored gelatin
1/2 teaspoon lemon juice
1 tablespoon grated onion
Dash of Tabasco sauce
1/2 cup Homemade Mayonnaise
  (page 39)

Combine the soup and 1/2 soup can cold water in a medium saucepan. Soften the gelatin in the remaining 1/2 soup can cold water. Heat the soup mixture over medium heat. Add the gelatin mixture, lemon juice, onion and Tabasco sauce; mix well. Cook until heated through; do not boil. Pour into an 8x8-inch glass dish. Chill, covered, until set. Cut into squares. Top each serving with a dollop of homemade mayonnaise.

"When my daughter was little she was into everything. I'd put her up on the counter in the kitchen when I was cooking and she would sit there and watch. She's just kind of picked up the knack for cooking …"
—Donna McCabe

Bleu Cheese Dressing

Yield: 3 cups

1 pint Hellman's mayonnaise
1/4 cup vinegar
2/3 cup vegetable oil
1/4 teaspoon garlic powder
Dash of white pepper
4 ounces bleu cheese, crumbled

Combine the mayonnaise, vinegar and oil in a large bowl; mix well. Stir in the garlic powder and white pepper. Add the bleu cheese; mix well. Pour into a serving container. Chill, covered, until serving time. May store for several weeks in the refrigerator.

Buttermilk Bleu Cheese Dressing

Yield: 5 quarts

1 gallon mayonnaise
1 cup vinegar
1 cup vegetable oil
1 1/2 cups buttermilk
2 envelopes Italian salad dressing mix
16 ounces bleu cheese, crumbled

Combine the mayonnaise, vinegar, oil and buttermilk in a large bowl; mix well. Add the Italian dressing mix; mix well. Stir in the crumbled bleu cheese. Pour into serving containers. Chill, covered, until serving time.

Curry French Dressing

Yield: 1 cup

1 teaspoon salt, or
    1/4 teaspoon onion salt
1/4 teaspoon celery salt
1/2 teaspoon (or more) sugar
1/2 teaspoon dry mustard
1/4 teaspoon curry powder
1/4 teaspoon pepper
1/4 cup cider vinegar mixed with
    a small amount of tarragon vinegar
Juice of 1 lemon, or to taste
3/4 cup vegetable oil

Combine the salt, celery salt, sugar, dry mustard, curry powder and pepper in a blender container. Add the vinegar and lemon juice; mix well. Add the oil gradually in a fine stream, processing constantly at high speed until smooth.

"We grew up in a fun household and we were a close family . . . We always had a house full of people, probably because Mother was a wonderful cook."
—Donna McCabe

French Dressing

Yield: 6 pints

4 cups vegetable oil

4 cups vinegar

1/3 cup Worcestershire sauce

1 (50-ounce) can tomato soup

2 cups sugar

3 teaspoons packed-in-water minced garlic

4 teaspoons ground mustard

4 teaspoons salt

2 teaspoons pepper

4 teaspoons paprika

1 1/2 teaspoons onion powder

Combine the oil, vinegar and Worcestershire sauce in a large bowl; mix well. Stir in the soup and sugar. Add the garlic; mix well. Combine the mustard, salt, pepper, paprika and onion powder in a small bowl; mix well. Add to the tomato soup mixture gradually, whisking constantly until well blended. Pour into serving containers. Chill, covered, until serving time.

"This is how I tell about mayonnaise. You just taste it to see if it's right. And if it doesn't taste right, you add a little bit more of something. It took me all day long to do that first batch of mayonnaise. After that I'd get up early in the morning, and make it—of course, I was young then."
—Mamie Strowd

SALADS

French Tarragon Dressing

Yield: 1 cup

1 tablespoon vinegar
1 tablespoon tarragon vinegar
Juice of 1/2 lemon
1 teaspoon salt
Onion juice to taste
Capers to taste
9 tablespoons vegetable oil

Combine the vinegar, tarragon vinegar, lemon juice, salt, onion juice and capers in a food processor container. Process until blended. Add the oil in a fine stream, processing constantly at high speed until completely blended.

Homemade Mayonnaise

Yield: 1 pint

3 egg yolks
1 teaspoon salt
Dash of red pepper
1 pint vegetable oil
1/2 teaspoon lemon juice
1 teaspoon vinegar

Beat the egg yolks, salt and red pepper in a large mixer bowl at medium speed until blended. Add the oil gradually, a drop at a time at first. As the mixture thickens, add the lemon juice and vinegar gradually. Note: Be sure to add the ingredients slowly or the mayonnaise may separate. If it does, start over with 1 more egg yolk and add the separated mixture slowly.

"Mother's mother taught her how to make mayonnaise. She started making it and selling it back in the Depression because she had to think of a way to bring some extra money into the family."
—Mamie Strowd

Poppy Seed Dressing

Yield: 1³/₄ cups

1/3 cup sugar
1/2 cup white vinegar
1 teaspoon salt
1 teaspoon dry mustard
1 teaspoon grated onion
1 cup vegetable oil
1 tablespoon poppy seeds

Combine the sugar, vinegar, salt, dry mustard and onion in a blender container; process on High for 20 seconds. Add the oil gradually in a fine stream, processing constantly at high speed until smooth. Stir in the poppy seeds.

Thousand Island Dressing

Yield: 3 pints

3 cups mayonnaise
1 cup mayonnaise-type salad
　dressing
2 cups catsup
1/2 cup sweet pickle relish
2 tablespoons lemon juice

Combine the mayonnaise, mayonnaise-type salad dressing and catsup in a large bowl; mix well. Stir in the relish and lemon juice. Pour into a serving container. Chill, covered, until serving time.

"Daddy would sometimes get a little money and come home and give Mama fifty cents. Even back then fifty cents wasn't a lot of money, but Mama would use it to put a meal on the table for eight people."

—Mamie Strowd

"The Lovelesses were good people from Centerville, a real nice couple."

—Stella Maynard,
Loveless owner 1957-1974

HISTORY OF THE LOVELESS III

The Loveless opened in 1951, when the post–World War II exodus of Americans along their roads was at its height. In an era before interstates, the U.S. highways and state roads—most of them two-lane and paved for the first time—were the beneficiaries of the postwar prosperity that meant Americans had more of everything, including appliances, cars, and money. We went south to Florida or west to the warmth of Arizona, Utah, and California. America was mobile, rich, powerful, and on top of the world. We seemed to have it all.

U.S. highways didn't bypass the towns of America like the interstates do now, creating "second cities" away from Main Street. No, highways like Route 66 were the Main Streets of America. Highway 100 ran right through the wealthy suburb of Belle Meade, continuing through Pasquo, Belle Vue, Fairview, and Centerville, all the way to the Mississippi.

The postwar decade was a time of intense restlessness in the American psyche. We no longer felt content to sit at home and observe the world. The 1950s were the decade of Ginsberg and Kerouac and *On the Road*; it was the decade of Elvis and Little Richard and the stirrings of rock and roll. It was the decade of Brown *vs.* the Board of Education. The 1950s were the years when America started to change.

Into this world of mobility and change and postwar prosperity stepped Lon and Annie Loveless—as unlikely a couple as there ever was to open a café on the route of the Great American Exodus. "Mr. Lon," as the locals in Hickman County still call him, was born in 1887 and died in 1961. Miss Annie was born in 1905 and lived until 1990. Both were children of the soil, native Middle Tennesseans.

It's worth dwelling a bit on the character of the couple who started this American landmark—for that's truly what the Loveless has become. It's been written about not only in the local press, but in such prestigious journals as *Gourmet* and *Esquire*.

For the first 40 years of his life, Lon Loveless followed the traditions of his ancestors in Hickman County. He farmed, going out every morning before the sun was up to sweat in the fields. Miss Annie, in the meantime, was learning how to cook, make jams and jellies, and "put up" the fruits and vegetables. She became a wonderful cook. Each of them married other people first.

Mr. Lon had a lot of interests: he loved baseball, country ham, politics, and square dancing. He became involved in local Democratic Party circles and in 1933, when the sheriff of Hickman County suddenly resigned, Lon was one of seventeen people who applied to the County Court to take the former sheriff's place. Sixteen other people thought they could do the job just as well, and it took seven ballots to pick the winner.

Mr. Lon was a good sheriff, folks remember, and a popular one, too. There was a law in Hickman County at that time that said no sheriff could be elected to more than three full consecutive terms. At the end of his third term, in 1938, Mr. Lon filed for re-election again, and that brought a reaction. A lawsuit was filed trying to stop him, but the local Chancery Court ruled that he had not served three complete terms. So he ran again and won again—and then stepped down. (Sheriffing ran in the family. Lon's son, Mayhew, was later elected to several terms as sheriff.)

Sometime during World War II, Mr. Lon and Miss Annie met. Both were single again and both were middle-aged. Nature followed its course and they got married. Mr. Lon didn't want to go back to farming and Miss Annie could cook up a storm, so they decided to open a restaurant. In fact, they opened several: the first was the Blue Front Cafe, located in an old building on the Centerville square that somebody had painted a bright sky blue. After World War II, they moved out Highway 100 near the Buffalo River and opened the first Loveless's. Then they moved back toward Lyles and opened the Beacon Light Tea Room. As the decade turned from the 1940s to the 1950s, they had another idea: move closer to Nashville.

The white clapboard place that houses the restaurant now was already in existence in 1951, doing business as the Harpeth Tea Room (since 1947) when Mr. Lon and Miss Annie decided they needed to be closer to Nashville to catch some of the outgoing and incoming traffic. So they bought the place, added a few rooms out back, put up the big blue-and-white neon sign, and went to work creating a Nashville institution.

continued on page 60

BREAKFAST

&

BREADS

Sausage Suzanne Brunch Casserole

Yield: 7 to 8 servings

1/2 pound mild sausage
4 slices bread, crusts trimmed
4 eggs, beaten
1 cup milk
1 teaspoon dry mustard
1 teaspoon salt
2 cups shredded Cheddar cheese

Brown the sausage in a skillet, stirring until crumbly and cooked through; drain. Tear the bread into bite-size pieces. Combine the sausage, bread, eggs, milk, dry mustard, salt and cheese in a bowl; mix well. Pour into a non-stick 2-quart casserole. Chill, covered, for 8 to 10 hours. Bake at 325 degrees for 50 minutes.

Sausage Cheese Balls

Yield: 10 dozen

1 pound mild sausage
1 pound hot sausage
4 to 5 cups shredded extra-sharp
   Cheddar cheese
4 cups baking mix

Allow the sausages and cheese to come to room temperature in a large bowl. Add the baking mix. Combine the mixture by hand until well mixed. Shape into small balls. Arrange on a nonstick baking sheet with sides. Bake at 350 degrees for 20 minutes or until cooked through.

"Tell anybody who's ever found lumps in their grits or gravy, or wrestled to get a roux just right, to just whip 'em with a whisk. It's the poor man's mixer."
—George McCabe (*Tennessean* interview, Feb. 9, 1994)

Sausage Roll-Ups

Yield: 9 dozen

2 pounds mild sausage
1 pound hot sausage
4 cups baking mix

Let the sausages come to room temperature in a bowl; mix well. Prepare a dough from the baking mix using package directions. Roll the dough very thin between 2 sheets of lightly floured waxed paper. Spread a thin layer of sausage over the dough to within 1/2 inch of the edges. Roll as for a jelly roll, removing the waxed paper. Chill, covered in waxed paper, for about 1 hour or until firm. Cut into 1/4-inch-thick pieces. Arrange on a nonstick baking sheet. Bake at 350 degrees for 15 to 20 minutes or until brown and sausage is cooked through. Serve immediately. May freeze unused portions.

"Princess Anne stood up there and talked to me for, oh, five or ten minutes when they got ready to leave. She said she didn't normally eat a big breakfast because she rode and it was pretty hard on her if she did."
—Donna McCabe
(*Milwaukee Journal* interview, Oct. 19, 1994)

Baked Crêpe

Yield: 1 crêpe

3 to 4 tablespoons butter or
    margarine
1/2 cup flour
1/2 cup milk
2 eggs
Nutmeg to taste

Melt the butter in the bottom of an ovenproof nonstick skillet. Pour a mixture of the flour, milk, eggs and nutmeg into the skillet. Bake at 400 degrees for 15 minutes.

Quick Coffee Cake

Yield: 9 servings

1 3/4 cups sifted flour
2 1/2 teaspoons baking powder
1/2 teaspoon salt
1/3 cup sugar
1/4 cup butter, softened
1 egg, well beaten
1/2 cup milk
1 teaspoon vanilla extract
3 tablespoons melted butter
1/3 cup sugar
1 tablespoon flour
1/2 teaspoon cinnamon

Sift the 1 3/4 cups flour, baking powder, salt and 1/3 cup sugar into a bowl. Cut in the 1/4 cup butter. Add the egg and milk; mix well. Stir in the vanilla. Spread the batter into a greased 9- or 10-inch baking pan. Brush the top with the 3 tablespoons melted butter. Sprinkle a mixture of 1/3 cup sugar, 1 tablespoon flour and the cinnamon over the top. Bake at 350 to 400 degrees for 25 to 30 minutes. Serve warm.

"... for a total Nashville experience, sit down to an old-fashioned Tennessee breakfast at the Loveless Café."
—*USA Weekend,*
May 1990

Sour Cream Coffee Cake

Yield: 10 servings

1/2 cup margarine, softened

1 cup sugar

1 teaspoon vanilla extract

2 eggs

1 cup sour cream

2 cups flour

1 teaspoon baking powder

1 teaspoon baking soda

1 teaspoon salt

3 tablespoons flour

3 tablespoons melted margarine

3/4 cup packed brown sugar

2 teaspoons cinnamon

3/4 cup chopped nuts

Cream 1/2 cup margarine and the sugar in a mixer bowl until light and fluffy. Beat in the vanilla and eggs. Add the sour cream alternately with a sifted mixture of the 2 cups flour, baking powder, baking soda and salt, mixing well after each addition. Pour half the batter into a greased and floured 9x13-inch baking pan. Combine the 3 tablespoons flour, 3 tablespoons melted margarine, brown sugar, cinnamon and nuts in a small bowl; mix well. Sprinkle half the brown sugar mixture over the batter in the pan. Spread the remaining batter over the top. Sprinkle with the remaining brown sugar mixture. Bake at 350 degrees for 25 to 30 minutes or until light brown.

"Just west of town on Highway 100, Loveless has garnered a national reputation for its classic breakfast layout."
—March Egerton,
Dallas Morning News,
Nov. 29, 1992

Stay-Up-All-Night Coffee Cake

Yield: 16 servings

3/4 cup chopped nuts
1 package frozen Parker House rolls
1 (4-ounce) package butterscotch
    instant pudding mix
1/2 cup packed brown sugar
1/2 cup melted margarine
2 teaspoons (or more) cinnamon

Sprinkle the nuts into the bottom of a greased bundt pan. Arrange the rolls evenly over the nuts. Sprinkle the dry pudding mix over the rolls. Combine the brown sugar, melted margarine and cinnamon in a small bowl; mix well. Spoon over the rolls. Place the bundt pan in a cold oven for 8 to 10 hours. Remove the bundt pan from the oven. Preheat the oven to 350 degrees. Return the bundt pan to the oven. Bake for 25 minutes.

Cinnamon Rolls

Yield: 12 to 15 servings

2 cups baking mix
1/2 cup milk
1/4 cup butter, softened
1 tablespoon cinnamon
1 tablespoon sugar

Combine the baking mix and milk in a medium bowl; mix well. Roll out 1/4 inch thick on a lightly floured surface. Spread with the butter. Sprinkle with a mixture of the cinnamon and sugar. Roll as for a jelly roll. Cut into 1/4-inch pieces; arrange cut side up in a baking pan. Bake at 425 degrees for 15 to 20 minutes or until brown.

"Old-timers will tell you that nothing tastes as good as food cooked in a cast-iron skillet on a wood stove. Well, modern Southern cooks are glad to be free from those wood-burning stoves, but they hung onto those skillets.

Banana Bread

Yield: 12 servings

3/4 cup sugar
1/3 cup vegetable oil
1 egg
2 to 3 ripe bananas, mashed
1/3 cup self-rising flour, sifted

Combine the sugar, oil, egg and bananas in a mixer bowl; mix well. Stir in the sifted self-rising flour. Pour into a nonstick loaf pan. Bake at 350 degrees for 1 hour or until a wooden pick inserted in the center comes out clean. Remove to a wire rack to cool.

Date-Nut Bread

Yield: 12 servings

1 1/2 cups boiling water
1 1/2 cups chopped dates
2 tablespoons butter
1 1/2 cups sugar
1 egg
2 3/4 cups flour
1 teaspoon baking soda
1 teaspoon salt
1 teaspoon cream of tartar
1 cup chopped walnuts

Pour the boiling water over the dates in a small bowl; let stand until cool. Cream the butter and sugar in a mixer bowl until light and fluffy. Beat in the egg. Add the cooled dates mixture. Add a sifted mixture of the flour, baking soda, salt and cream of tartar; mix well. Stir in the walnuts. Pour into a nonstick loaf pan. Bake at 350 degrees for 1 1/4 hours. Remove to a wire rack to cool.

One lady . . . said that she used the same cast-iron skillet for 35 years. She had raised all of her children and part of her grandchildren out of that skillet, and when it broke, an era was gone. She bought another one, but of course, it didn't seem the same."
—Michael Grissom, *Southern by the Grace of God*

Wheat Muffins

Yield: 10 to 12 servings

1½ cups sifted flour
¼ cup baking powder
½ teaspoon salt
1 teaspoon sugar
1 egg, beaten
1 cup milk
5 tablespoons melted butter

Sift the sifted flour, baking powder, salt and sugar into a mixer bowl. Add a mixture of the egg and milk; mix well. Stir in the melted butter. Spoon into greased muffin cups. Bake at 450 degrees until brown.

Blackberry Preserves

Yield: variable

10 pounds fresh blackberries
5 pounds sugar

Rinse the blackberries; remove and discard any stems. Pour the blackberries into a large saucepan. Add the sugar; mix well. Bring the mixture to a boil, stirring until the sugar dissolves; reduce heat. Cook until the mixture is thickened and of jam consistency, stirring frequently to prevent the mixture from sticking to the saucepan. Ladle the mixture into hot sterilized jars, leaving a ½-inch headspace; seal with 2-piece lids. Process in a boiling water bath for 10 minutes.

"Mrs. Loveless came up with the jam recipes . . . when I was there and when Mrs. Loveless was there, we made our blackberry jam out of the berry that was picked out in the woods, the wild blackberry. It wasn't tame."
—Stella Maynard, owner 1957–74

Peach Preserves

Yield: variable

36 pounds sliced peaches packed
   in water
10 pounds sugar

*Cook the undrained peaches in a
large saucepan over medium heat for
2 hours, stirring frequently. Add the
sugar, stirring until the sugar dissolves.
Cook for 1 to 2 hours longer or until
mixture is of desired consistency. Ladle
the mixture into hot sterilized jars,
leaving a $1/2$-inch headspace; seal with
2-piece lids. Process in a boiling water
bath for 10 minutes.*

"We cook jam
every week . . . I
mean, it's fresh.
We're making it all
the time."
—Donna McCabe

Strawberry Preserves

Yield: variable

3 cups sugar
2 cups strawberries
$1/2$ lemon, thinly sliced

*Combine the sugar, strawberries and
lemon slices in a large saucepan. Bring
to a boil; reduce heat. Cook for 10 to
12 minutes. Discard the lemon slices.
Skim the foam with a spoon. Remove
from heat. Let stand for 8 to 10 hours.
Ladle the mixture into hot sterilized
jars, leaving a $1/2$-inch headspace; seal
with 2-piece lids. Process in a boiling
water bath for 10 minutes.*

Corn Bread

Yield: 8 to 9 servings

1 cup buttermilk
1 cup cornmeal
$1/4$ teaspoon baking soda
Salt to taste
1 egg, beaten
$3/4$ teaspoon baking powder
2 tablespoons vegetable oil

> "I've got to have buttermilk for corn bread."
>
> —Donna McCabe

Stir the buttermilk into the cornmeal in a small bowl. Add the baking soda and salt; mix well. Stir in the beaten egg. Add the baking powder and oil; mix well. Pour into a nonstick baking pan. Bake at 425 degrees until brown. May substitute melted shortening or butter for the oil.

Corn Light Bread

Yield: 24 servings

1 quart sour buttermilk
1 cup sugar
2 cups self-rising cornmeal
1 cup self-rising flour
2 tablespoons melted lard

Combine the buttermilk, sugar, cornmeal, flour and lard in a mixer bowl; mix well. Pour the batter into 2 greased loaf pans. Bake at 350 degrees for 1 hour. Remove to a wire rack to cool immediately. Let stand until cool. Cover the bread loaves in plastic wrap. May store in the refrigerator for up to a week and may reheat before serving.

Corn Muffins

Yield: 5 large muffins

1/2 cup cornmeal

1/4 teaspoon salt

1/2 cup boiling water

1/4 cup milk

1 egg, beaten

1 teaspoon baking powder

1 teaspoon melted butter

Sift the cornmeal and salt into a small bowl. Pour in the boiling water; mix well. Add the milk all at once; mix well. Stir in the beaten egg. Add the baking powder and butter; mix well. Spoon into 5 large nonstick muffin cups. Bake at 425 degrees until brown.

Hush Puppies

Yield: 12 servings

1 cup cornmeal

1 teaspoon baking powder

1/2 teaspoon salt

1/4 teaspoon sugar

1 egg, beaten

1/3 cup milk

1 tablespoon grated onion

Sift the cornmeal, baking powder, salt and sugar into a bowl. Add the egg, milk and onion; mix well. Pour enough oil in a heavy saucepan to measure 3/4 inch; heat to boiling. Spoon the batter by level tablespoonfuls into the hot oil. Cook until brown on both sides; drain. Serve immediately.

"We threw ourselves into a big plate of real country ham and fresh eggs with redeye gravy and couldn't resist several servings of the Loveless' famous scratch biscuits and the homemade blackberry and peach preserves."
—Angeline Goreau, *Gourmet*, April 1996

Aunt Kat's Spoon Bread

Yield: 9 servings

2 cups milk
1 tablespoon (heaping) margarine
1/2 to 1 teaspoon salt
3/4 cup cornmeal
4 egg yolks
4 egg whites

Scald the milk with the margarine in the top of a double boiler. Mix the salt and cornmeal with enough water to make a paste in a bowl. Beat the egg yolks in a mixer bowl. Mix in the cornmeal mixture. Add to the milk in the top of the double boiler. Cook until thickened, stirring constantly. Remove from heat; place in a pan of cold water. Beat the egg whites until stiff in a mixer bowl; fold into the cornmeal mixture. Pour into a greased 2-quart baking dish. Place in a large skillet of water. Place in a preheated 350 degree oven. Bake for 20 to 30 minutes.

"One of the pleasures of breakfast when you travel is that it's a meal that a lot of local people eat out. They go home for supper and may eat lunch on the job, but a lot of people start the day going to a café in small-town America."
—Michael Stern, *USA Today*, May 12, 1993

Egg Bread

Yield: 10 servings

2 cups cornmeal
2 eggs
1 1/2 cups milk
1/2 teaspoon salt
Pinch of baking soda
2 tablespoons baking powder

Mix all the ingredients in a mixer bowl. Drop 10 spoonfuls of batter into a preheated cast-iron skillet greased with bacon drippings. Bake at 400 degrees for 25 minutes.

Bread Loaves

Yield: 24 servings

1 medium potato, peeled
1/3 cup shortening
1/3 cup sugar
1 teaspoon salt
1 egg, beaten
1 envelope dry yeast or 1/2 cake yeast
1/2 cup lukewarm water
41/2 to 5 cups flour, sifted twice
2 tablespoons melted butter

Cook the potato until tender in boiling water in a saucepan; drain, reserving 1 cup of the cooking liquid. Mash the potato in a small bowl. Cream the shortening, sugar and salt in a large mixer bowl. Add the mashed potato; mix well. Dissolve the yeast in the lukewarm water in a small bowl; add to the potato mixture. Add 2 cups of the sifted flour alternately with the reserved cooking liquid, mixing well after each addition. Add the remaining flour gradually; mix well. Knead on a floured surface until smooth and elastic. Place in a greased bowl, turning to coat the surface. Let rise, covered with a damp cloth, in a warm place until doubled in bulk. Punch the dough down. Divide the dough; shape the dough into 2 loaves in 2 greased loaf pans. Let rise, covered, until doubled in bulk. Brush with the melted butter. Bake at 350 degrees for 25 minutes or until golden brown. Remove from the pan. Cool on a wire rack.

"... we suggest you drive out to the Loveless, where you will have the best meal in town, at one of the great undiscovered restaurants of the south."
—Jane and Michael Stern, *Good Food*

Refrigerator Rolls

Yield: 40 servings

1/2 cup shortening
1/2 cup sugar
3 cups boiling water
1 cake yeast
6 cups sifted flour
1 tablespoon salt
Melted butter

Combine the shortening and sugar in a large mixer bowl; mix well. Pour the boiling water over the top. Break the yeast into the water mixture when water is lukewarm. Let stand until the yeast rises to the top. Stir in the flour and salt with a spoon; mix well. Let rise, covered, in a warm place until doubled in bulk. Punch the dough down. Cover the bowl with a sheet of waxed paper. Place a plate on top of the waxed paper. Refrigerate until ready to use. Roll 1/2 inch thick on a lightly floured surface; cut with a biscuit cutter. Fold over; place on a buttered baking sheet. Let rise, covered, in a warm place until doubled in bulk. Drizzle generously with the melted butter before baking. Bake at 425 degrees for 15 minutes or until golden brown. Note: For clover-leaf rolls, shape the dough into 1-inch balls. Place 3 balls into each buttered muffin cup.

"On a scale of one to ten, my breakfast came in at about a fourteen."
—Jefferson Morgan, *Bon Appetit*, July 1987

"People came just to hear him talk . . ."

—Ed Dotson,
Historian of Hickman County,
speaking of Lon Loveless

HISTORY OF THE LOVELESS IV

Nobody knows whether the Lovelesses were aware that the Natchez Trace Parkway was making its way through Pasquo, and what it might mean for their business. Early Department of the Interior maps showed clearly enough that the road was meant to end almost at the hotel's front door. Maybe the Lovelesses thought that if they bought the hotel and held onto it long enough they could make something out of it.

Nashville didn't have a lot of hotel space in the 1950s. Travelers didn't have much to choose from, only the big old downtown hotels like the Hermitage and the Maxwell House. Nashville wasn't yet Music City USA; it was a sleepy Southern capital city with a population of barely 300,000 people. They called it "The Athens of the South." People might travel to Nashville to see the Parthenon or to enroll their kid at Vanderbilt University or Peabody College, and that's about it. There was no Opryland and no Second Avenue. Although the Ryman Auditorium was already in full flower as the home of the Grand Ole Opry, country music hadn't yet taken hold in the national consciousness. The stars of the Opry in 1951—Roy Acuff, Ernest Tubb, and Bill Monroe—were not very well known past a 100-mile radius of Nashville

(Acuff made a couple of Hollywood pictures that nobody ever saw). The only country music people with national reputations were a Centerville girl named Sarah Ophelia Colley who had meandered up Highway 100, graduated from the exclusive Ward-Belmont Finishing School for Girls, then created a comic Opry character named Minnie Pearl; and a sad-eyed troubadour from Mobile named Hank Williams, who in 1951 was in his twenties and had only two more years to live. Hank Williams would give the Opry its first cult hero and begin the process of melding hillbilly music into the popular culture of material plenty and psychological famine.

Buying the Harpeth Tea Room was a challenge for Lon and Annie Loveless and one that they tackled with all the enthusiasm of kids, even though Mr. Lon was already in his 60s when they moved in. Right away, they knew what kind of food they wanted to serve. The Beacon Light had been known for its ham and biscuits, so they brought their recipes with them. Mr. Lon would scour the countryside looking for the best places to buy his hams. Then he would slice them himself, taking care to pat each ham with his hands to bring out the natural fluids. Miss Annie took care of the kitchen and the recipes, buying the freshest vegetables, tracking out in the woods for the wild blackberries to make the jam, and—most important—coming up with the secret biscuit recipe.

The Loveless earned a reputation for good company and good food. Mr. Lon and Miss Annie piled the biscuits on a plate and kept 'em coming. Mr. Lon greeted each visitor like a long-lost friend.

"People came just to hear him talk," said Ed Dotson, county historian of Hickman County. "He had a wonderful voice and he just loved telling stories. He loved everything there was about being part of a community.

He would call all the sets at the local square dances and he would go to the local baseball games and just yell and shout. He and his brothers were all great baseball fans. If one of their sons made a good play, they bragged on him; if he made an error, they denied it ever took place."

As promising as the 1950s were for the entrepreneurial spirit, Mr. Lon and Miss Annie waited just a little bit late in life to see their creation become one of the most famous eateries in the nation. By 1957 Mr. Lon was 70 years old and beginning to suffer from heart trouble. He and Miss Annie wanted to stay in the restaurant business, somehow, but they also wanted to go back home. So they sold the café and motel to Stella and Cordell Maynard in 1960. As part of the sale, Lon and Annie agreed that they couldn't use their own name if they started another restaurant. They went back to Lyles and operated The Beacon Light again. Shortly before Mr. Lon died in 1961, they started yet another place in the community of Fairfield.

"They were a real nice couple," says Stella Maynard, "and I think selling their place affected Mr. Lon. About three months after they sold it to us, he had a heart attack."

After Mr. Lon died, Miss Annie offered her services to Stella Maynard. Maynard remembers that both of them worked long hours, perfecting recipes in the kitchen, and most of all, tramping through the woods looking for wild blackberries.

"We didn't use any tame blackberries," Stella Maynard says. "It would take some of the tang out of the taste if we did."

continued on page 80

MEATS

Beef Pot Roast with Gravy

Yield: 5 to 6 servings

1 (2- to 3-pound) boneless chuck
    roast
1 tablespoon vegetable oil
4 cups water
4 beef bouillon cubes
4 to 5 carrots, peeled, each cut into
    3 pieces
4 to 5 potatoes, peeled, cut into
    large pieces
2 tablespoons flour
1 cup water
Garlic salt or seasoned salt to taste
Black pepper to taste

Sear the roast in the oil in an oven-proof roaster pan until brown on both sides. Add the 4 cups water and bouillon cubes. Bake, covered, at 400 degrees for 1 1/2 hours. Arrange the carrots and potatoes around the meat. Cook for 30 minutes longer or until the meat and vegetables are tender. Transfer the meat and vegetables to a serving dish. Add a mixture of flour and 1 cup water to the hot pan drippings in the roaster pan; whip until thickened, adding water if needed.

"I've got . . . an aluminum roaster that belonged to Mother. It is the best thing you could ever cook meat in, because it makes it so tender."

—Mamie Strowd

Pot Roast

Yield: 6 servings

1 (2- to 3-pound) chuck roast
2 quarts water
1 medium onion, sliced
4 ribs celery, cut into 2-inch pieces
2 beef bouillon cubes
Garlic powder to taste
Salt and pepper to taste
5 to 6 Idaho potatoes, peeled,
    cut into large pieces
6 carrots, cut into halves

Cook the roast in an electric skillet at 350 degrees until brown on both sides. Add the water. Arrange the onion slices on top of the meat and the celery around the meat. Drop the bouillon cubes in the water. Season the meat with the garlic powder, salt and pepper. Simmer, covered, for 1 hour. Arrange the potatoes and carrots around the meat. Cook for 1 to 2 hours longer or until the meat and vegetables are tender. Transfer the meat and vegetables to a serving dish. May thicken the remaining pan drippings with a mixture of flour and water for gravy.

"We are real careful to pick out the better meats . . . that's what makes the food good, because we use better foods and good products."
—Donna McCabe

Pepper Steak

Yield: 8 servings

1/2 cup chopped onion
2 green bell peppers, cut into strips
1/2 cup butter
2 pounds round steak, cut into
    8 pieces
1/8 teaspoon garlic powder
1 (16-ounce) can chopped tomatoes
1 beef bouillon cube, crushed
1 teaspoon cornstarch
1/4 cup water
3 tablespoons soy sauce
1 teaspoon sugar
1 teaspoon salt

Sauté the onion and green peppers in the butter in a large skillet for 2 minutes or until the vegetables are tender; drain. Remove the vegetables to a bowl. Arrange the meat in the pan drippings in the skillet. Sprinkle with the garlic powder. Cook until the meat is brown on both sides. Pour a mixture of the tomatoes and crushed bouillon over the top. Bring to a boil; reduce heat. Simmer for 10 minutes. Add a mixture of the cornstarch, water, soy sauce, sugar and salt. Cook until the tomato mixture is thickened and the meat is tender. Stir in the onion and green peppers.

"My daughter can fix the best meal out of nothing of anybody I ever saw. She'll get a little piece of meat, and by the time you sit down you will find a wonderful meal on the table."

—Donna McCabe

Beef Stew

Yield: 12 to 15 servings

1 (4-pound) boneless chuck roast,
    cut into cubes
3 large onions, chopped
2 tablespoons vegetable oil
4 ribs celery, chopped
1 1/2 gallons water
3 bay leaves
3 tablespoons Worcestershire sauce
1 (15-ounce) can tomato sauce
1 tablespoon A-1 Steak Sauce
1/2 cup catsup
4 potatoes, peeled, cubed
5 to 6 carrots, peeled, sliced
1 (16-ounce) can green peas
Salt and pepper to taste

Sear the meat and onions in the oil in a large stockpot. Add the celery. Cook for 5 minutes longer. Pour in the water. Add the bay leaves. Stir in a mixture of the Worcestershire sauce, tomato sauce, A-1 Sauce and catsup. Bring to a boil; reduce heat. Cook over medium heat until the meat is tender. Add the potatoes, carrots and peas. Cook until the vegetables are tender. Season with the salt and pepper. Remove and discard the bay leaves before serving.

"I experimented with the stew the other day and it turned out good . . . Mamie's husband made such good stew, and it really tasted almost like his. Even George agreed that my beef stew was pretty much like his dad's, so I'm going to write that one down."
—Donna McCabe

City Chicken (Veal)

Yield: 6 servings

1 (2-pound) boneless veal shoulder

1/2 cup fine cracker crumbs

1/2 cup crumbled cornflakes

1 teaspoon salt

1 teaspoon paprika

3/4 teaspoon poultry seasoning or
  thyme

1/2 teaspoon MSG

Dash of pepper

1 egg, lightly beaten

2 tablespoons milk

2 to 3 tablespoons shortening

1 chicken bouillon cube

Cut the veal into 1 1/2-inch cubes. Spear the veal cubes onto 6 skewers. Combine the cracker crumbs, cornflake crumbs, salt, paprika, poultry seasoning, MSG and pepper in a flat dish; mix well. Dip the skewers of meat into a mixture of the egg and milk in a bowl; roll in the crumb mixture, coating all sides of the meat. Heat the shortening in a large skillet with a lid. Place the skewers of coated veal in the heated shortening. Brown the veal on all sides. Dissolve the bouillon cube in 3/4 cup hot water in a small bowl. Pour the bouillon mixture over the veal. Simmer, tightly covered, for 1 hour or until tender or done to taste; or bake, covered tightly, in a large baking dish at 350 degrees for 1 hour or until done to taste.

"To finish off a country tour of Nashville, try an authentic down-home restaurant like the one at the Loveless Motel."
—Rick Mashburn, *Travel and Leisure*, November 1989

Beefy Rice Casserole

Yield: 4 servings

1 pound ground beef
3 tablespoons butter
1 cup uncooked rice
1 medium onion, finely chopped
1 green bell pepper, finely chopped
1 (10-ounce) can tomato soup
2 soup cans water

Sauté the meat in 1 tablespoon of the butter in a large skillet until brown and crumbly; drain. Mix the meat with the rice in a 2-quart baking dish. Sauté the onion and green pepper in the remaining butter in the skillet until tender; drain. Add the soup and water; mix well. Pour over the meat mixture in the baking dish. Bake, covered, at 350 degrees for 1 to 1 1/2 hours, adding water as needed.

"Loveless Restaurant, the real McCoy of Southern cooking . . ."
—*USA Today*, August 1990

Suppertime Beef Casserole

Yield: 4 servings

1 (7-ounce) package macaroni and
    cheese dinner
1 pound ground beef
1 clove of garlic, chopped
1 (10-ounce) can onion soup
Salt and pepper to taste

Prepare the macaroni and cheese using package directions. Brown the ground beef with the garlic in a skillet, stirring until the ground beef is crumbly; drain. Add the soup and prepared macaroni and cheese; mix well. Season with the salt and pepper. Spoon the mixture into a 2-quart casserole. Bake at 350 degrees for 30 minutes. May substitute garlic powder for the fresh garlic.

"But there's a little bit something different about everything we cook . . . Donna might put a little bit something different in hers or I might put a little bit something different in mine."
—Mamie Strowd

Chili

Yield: 8 servings

2 pounds ground beef
1 onion, chopped
2 tablespoons chopped garlic
1 tablespoon vegetable oil
3 cups water
1½ tablespoons salt
3 tablespoons paprika
3 tablespoons chili powder
2 (15-ounce) cans chili beans

Brown the ground beef with the onion and garlic in the oil in a large saucepan, stirring until the ground beef is crumbly and the vegetables are tender; drain. Add the water; mix well. Stir in the salt, paprika and chili powder. Cook over low heat for 3 hours. Add the chili beans; mix well. Cook until heated through. May serve over spaghetti or tamales.

"Mamie has more recipes than I do because I've had to stop and do some other things while she's writing down recipes ... but we're getting some really good old ones."

—Donna McCabe

Lasagna

Yield: 8 to 10 servings

2 cups cottage cheese
1 pound ground beef
1/2 pound sausage
1 (6-ounce) can tomato paste
1 (8-ounce) can tomato sauce
Italian seasoning to taste
8 lasagna noodles, cooked, drained
2 cups shredded mozzarella cheese
1/4 cup grated Parmesan cheese

Drain any excess liquid from the cottage cheese. Cook the ground beef and sausage in a large skillet until brown and cooked through; drain. Add the tomato paste, tomato sauce and Italian seasoning; mix well. Layer the lasagna noodles, meat sauce, cottage cheese, mozzarella cheese and Parmesan cheese 1/2 at a time in a greased 9x13-inch baking dish. Bake at 275 degrees until bubbly. Remove from the oven. Let stand for 10 minutes before serving.

"Most of our recipes are pretty close, actually. Except Mamie's a better cook than I am."
—Donna McCabe

Meat Loaf

Yield: 4 to 6 servings

1¹/₂ pounds ground chuck or
  ground round
1 egg
1 medium onion, chopped
¹/₂ green bell pepper, chopped
Salt and pepper to taste
1 (16-ounce) can tomato sauce

Combine the ground chuck, egg, onion, green pepper, salt and pepper in a large bowl; mix well. Stir in half the tomato sauce. Shape into a loaf in a glass baking dish. Pour the remaining tomato sauce over the top. Bake, covered, at 350 degrees for 1 to 1¹/₂ hours or until cooked through.

"There are no prepackaged ingredients whatever in anything Mamie or I cook."

—Donna McCabe

Spaghetti

Yield: 4 servings

1 pound ground chuck
1 medium onion, chopped
1 green bell pepper, chopped
1 (16-ounce) can chopped tomatoes
1 (8-ounce) can tomato sauce
1 envelope McCormick's Spaghetti
    Sauce Mix
1 teaspoon Italian seasoning
1 tablespoon Worcestershire sauce
12 ounces uncooked vermicelli

Brown the ground chuck with the onion and green pepper in a large skillet, stirring until the ground chuck is crumbly and the vegetables are tender; drain. Add the tomatoes, tomato sauce, Spaghetti Sauce Mix, Italian seasoning and Worcestershire sauce; mix well. Cook over low heat for 1 hour. Cook the vermicelli using package directions; drain. Ladle the spaghetti sauce over the cooked vermicelli on serving plates. Serve with French bread.

"As we make a pot of spaghetti, we'll write down how much of this we put in it and that, and how much more we need to add."

—Mamie Strowd

Spaghetti for a Crowd

Yield: 10 to 12 servings

2 pounds lean ground beef
1 rib celery, chopped
1 large onion, chopped
1 small green bell pepper, chopped
1 clove of garlic, pressed through a
    garlic press
1 (28-ounce) can chopped tomatoes
1 (10-ounce) can tomato paste
1 (4-ounce) can sliced mushrooms
1/4 teaspoon salt
1/4 teaspoon pepper
2 tablespoons Worcestershire sauce
1 tablespoon Italian seasoning
2 pounds thin spaghetti
Grated Parmesan cheese to taste

Brown the ground beef with the celery, onion, green pepper and garlic in a large skillet over medium heat, stirring constantly until the ground beef is crumbly and the vegetables are tender; drain. Add the tomatoes, tomato paste and mushrooms; mix well. Stir in the salt, pepper, Worcestershire sauce and Italian seasoning. Reduce heat to low. Cook for 1 hour longer, stirring occasionally. Cook the spaghetti using package directions; drain. Ladle the hot sauce over the cooked spaghetti on serving plates. Sprinkle with the Parmesan cheese.

"Even when I'm off, I'm not off. If I'm off, I'm doing things for the restaurant . . . I like it, I really don't mind working. I have never minded working."
—Donna McCabe

Ham and Egg Casserole

Yield: 4 to 6 servings

2 cups chopped ham
4 hard-cooked eggs, sliced
1 (4-ounce) can sliced mushrooms,
    drained
1 (10-ounce) can cream of
    mushroom soup
1 (10-ounce) can cream of
    celery soup
1/2 to 1 soup can milk
1/2 pound medium Cheddar cheese,
    shredded

Layer the ham, eggs and mushrooms in a 2-quart casserole. Pour a mixture of the soups and milk over the top. Sprinkle with the cheese. Bake at 350 degrees until bubbly and the cheese is melted. May substitute mushroom pieces and stems for the sliced mushrooms.

Raisin Sauce

Yield: 2 cups

3 whole cloves
2 lemons, thinly sliced
2 cups sugar
2 cups vinegar
1 cup raisins

Combine the cloves, lemon slices, sugar, vinegar and raisins in a small saucepan; mix well. Bring to a boil; reduce heat. Cook for 10 minutes, stirring frequently. Serve with sugar-cured ham.

"My husband and I used to get in the car and drive all over Tennessee and Kentucky looking for hams. We sometimes stopped at fifty different places.

Pepper Jelly

Yield: 6 ($^1/_2$-pints)

1 cup chopped green bell peppers
1 cup chopped hot green peppers
7$^1/_2$ cups sugar
1$^1/_2$ cups (5% acid strength) white
  vinegar
2 (3-ounce) packages liquid fruit
  pectin
Paraffin

Combine the green peppers, hot green peppers, sugar and vinegar in a Dutch oven. Bring to a boil; reduce heat. Cook for 6 minutes, stirring frequently. Stir in the fruit pectin. Cook for 3 minutes longer, stirring frequently. Remove from the heat. Skim off the foam using a metal spoon. Pour the jelly into 6 hot, sterilized half-pint jars, leaving $^1/_2$ inch headspace. Cover with a $^1/_8$-inch layer of paraffin; seal with 2-piece lids. Process in a boiling water bath for 10 minutes.

The customers would say, 'That's the best country ham I've ever had. I don't know what y'all do to it, but it's the best I've ever had.'"
—Donna McCabe

Aunt Kat's Barbecue Sauce

Yield: 1 cup

1/2 cup vinegar
1/2 cup water
2 tablespoons catsup
1 tablespoon chili powder
Red pepper to taste
2 tablespoons butter

Combine the vinegar, water, catsup, chili powder, red pepper and butter in a small saucepan. Bring to a boil; reduce heat. Simmer until well blended, stirring frequently.

Barbecue Sauce

Yield: 6 pints

6 tablespoons brown sugar
Juice of 1/2 lemon
10 ounces Worcestershire sauce
1/2 cup Wright's liquid smoke
Garlic to taste
6 (32-ounce) bottles Hunt's catsup

Combine the brown sugar, lemon juice, Worcestershire sauce, liquid smoke and garlic in a large saucepan. Empty the catsup bottles into the brown sugar mixture. Add about 1 inch of water to each emptied catsup bottle; close each bottle. Shake well; open the bottles and add the contents to the brown sugar mixture in the saucepan. Bring to a boil; reduce heat. Simmer for 45 minutes to 1 hour. Serve with ribs or chicken.

"Ham was the most popular dish. My husband was really particular about his ham."
—Stella Maynard, owner 1957–1974

"Comprising only one percent of American highways, the interstate system has opened a lot of road to the dawdler. And a lot of space: the billboards have followed the traveler . . . I came to a ramshackle place called Smitty's Trading Post. Smitty was a merchant of relics . . ."

—William Least Heat Moon,
Blue Highways

HISTORY
OF THE
LOVELESS
V

Just like William Least Heat Moon's run-down Smitty's, the Loveless is a place of relics. From the rickety old whitewashed bridge over the ditch out front to the concrete porch waiting room where customers linger over the autographed photographs of the stars who've come to visit—Willard Scott, Jimmy Buffet, almost every star of the Opry—the Loveless is a place of relics of an age that is not so very far away.

In the 1950s, with the cars rolling and the highways booming and Americans wanting to see America, the Loveless seemed just one of a million roadside attractions. You can go to flea markets these days and buy packs of old postcards that show what things were like in pre-prepackaged America, when entrepreneurs opened strange and exotic restaurants along the roads designed to get the automobile traveler to stop. If the Loveless didn't have the cachet it has today, that's because back then it wasn't as rare. Motor courts and restaurants dotted the nation's highways; neon signs advertised home-cooked meals. It was only later, in an age of generic fast food and rapid transit, that the uniqueness of that period has come to be appreciated.

The big blue and red neon sign that Mr. Lon and Miss Annie erected in front of the Loveless is still the same, although it has been repaired once or twice. It's as American now as baseball: a symbol of the vim and vigor of a society on the rise, full of confidence and entrepreneurial daring, of a time when a middle-aged couple could take their dreams and start again.

Like Lon and Annie, Cordell and Stella Maynard had lived a lifetime before entering the restaurant business. They got interested in the Loveless after their son saw in the paper that Mr. Lon and Miss Annie intended to sell it. Stella had worked at Genesco for thirty years and Cordell had been at Foster-Creighton crane operators.

Back then the business was so much more than a restaurant. Travelers would stop, eat a meal, and check into the motel. That meant not only food preparation, but fresh bed linens and towels and room cleanings as well.

"We lived in a Spando trailer out there behind the café," Stella says. "It was a lot of work. I was in the kitchen from 8 AM to 11 PM every day. Then we'd close up and go back to the trailer."

In the early 1960s, travelers began to come to Nashville in increasing numbers. Patsy Cline, Eddie Arnold, and Porter Waggoner (with his sequined suits) were mainstays at the Opry. Younger names—Tom T. Hall, Willie Nelson, and Waylon Jennings—were beginning to be heard.

HISTORY
OF THE
LOVELESS
V

Country music may not have been the favorite in New York or Los Angeles yet, but in the hamlets of central and southern Kentucky, the Alabama, Mississippi, and Georgia border counties, eastern Arkansas, and even as far as Oklahoma where talents like Merle Haggard could pick up the clear channel signal of 650 WSM-AM on the radio dial, Nashville was becoming the lodestone, the place where the roads converged. Fame and fortune could be had for anyone who could twang a guitar, strum a banjo, or wail a love song into the microphone.

The music hopefuls would crowd into Tootsie's down on Lower Broad looking for a break. Then they'd look for a place to stay. Mama and Daddy and the kids would come to town and put up at places like the Loveless, then stand in line for tickets to the Opry. The lines stretched for blocks in downtown Nashville.

"It wasn't just the music people who came," says Stella. "The last Sunday I was there, I served 836 people. It was booked all the time, particularly the motel. We had people call first, and I'd go to the Grand Ole Opry and get them tickets."

continued on page 100

POULTRY

&

SEAFOOD

Chicken à la King

Yield: 10 to 12 servings

1 (7- to 8-pound) chicken
1 (6-ounce) can sliced mushrooms, drained
1 (2-ounce) jar chopped pimentos, drained
4 green or red bell peppers, chopped
Salt to taste
Pepper to taste
Cayenne pepper to taste
Paprika to taste
Cream Sauce
12 hard-cooked eggs, chopped

Rinse the chicken. Combine the chicken with enough water to cover in a saucepan. Cook until tender. Drain, reserving the broth for the Cream Sauce; chop the chicken, discarding the skin and bones. Combine the chopped chicken, mushrooms, pimentos, and green peppers in a large bowl; mix well. Stir in the salt, pepper, cayenne pepper and paprika. Add the chicken mixture to the Cream Sauce in the large saucepan. Add the chopped eggs. Cook over medium heat until heated through, stirring frequently. Serve hot.

"... the quintessential country-Western eatery with homemade hot biscuits brought to the table throughout the meal."
—*USA Today*, May 12, 1993

Cream Sauce

1/2 cup butter
1 teaspoon flour
1 (12-ounce) can evaporated milk
1 3/4 cups reserved broth

Melt the butter in a large saucepan. Add the flour; mix well. Stir in the evaporated milk and broth. Cook over medium heat until thickened, stirring constantly.

Chicken Breasts with Wild Rice

Yield: 8 servings

1 cup uncooked wild rice, rinsed, drained
1 (10-ounce) can cream of celery soup
1 (10-ounce) can cream of mushroom soup
1 soup can milk
4 whole chicken breasts, split, boned
1 envelope dry onion soup mix

Sprinkle the rice over the bottom of a greased 2-quart baking dish. Combine the soups and milk in a small saucepan. Cook over low heat until smooth, stirring constantly. Rinse the chicken and pat dry. Arrange the chicken over the rice. Sprinkle with the dry soup mix. Pour the soup mixture evenly over the top. Bake, covered tightly with foil, at 250 degrees for 2 hours.

"This pleasingly quaint café . . . is a living piece of Nashville's past." —Brian Mansfield, *Spirit*, May 1990

Chicken and Broccoli Casserole

Yield: 6 to 8 servings

1 (3-pound) chicken
1 (16-ounce) package frozen chopped broccoli, thawed
1 (10-ounce) can cream of mushroom soup
1 (10-ounce) can cream of chicken soup
2 cups shredded Cheddar cheese
1/2 cup bread crumbs

Rinse the chicken. Combine the chicken with enough water to cover in a saucepan. Cook until tender; drain. Chop the chicken, discarding the skin and bones. Combine the chopped chicken, broccoli and soups together in a bowl; mix well. Spoon the chicken mixture into a 2-quart casserole. Layer the cheese and bread crumbs over the top. Bake at 400 degrees for 30 minutes or until bubbly.

Chicken Casserole Supreme

Yield: 6 to 8 servings

1 (2½-pound) chicken
1 (10-ounce) can cream of mushroom
 soup
1 (10-ounce) can cream of chicken
 soup
3 hard-cooked eggs, chopped
½ cup mayonnaise
1½ teaspoons lemon juice
1½ cups chopped celery
½ cup slivered almonds
½ cup crushed potato chips

Rinse the chicken. Combine the chicken with enough water to cover in a saucepan. Cook until tender; drain. Chop the chicken, discarding the skin and bones. Combine the chicken, soups, hard-cooked eggs, mayonnaise, lemon juice, celery and almonds in a large bowl; mix well. Spoon into a 2-quart casserole. Bake at 400 degrees for 30 minutes or until bubbly. Sprinkle the potato chips over the top before serving.

"We were from a large family. There were six children, and of course, Mother and Daddy. We had three older brothers and an older sister and we had a good time growing up.

Chicken and Green Bean Casserole

Yield: 8 to 10 servings

6 to 8 boneless skinless chicken
    breasts
2 (16-ounce) cans French-style
    green beans, drained
16 ounces cream cheese, softened
2 cups milk
1 (10-ounce) can cream of
    mushroom soup
1/4 teaspoon garlic salt
1 tablespoon onion powder
1 (3-ounce) can French-fried
    onions

Rinse the chicken and pat dry. Cut the chicken into strips; arrange in the bottom of a 9x13-inch casserole. Spoon the green beans over the chicken. Combine the cream cheese, milk and soup in a small mixer bowl; mix well. Add the garlic salt and onion powder. Pour over the green beans. Top with the French-fried onions. Bake at 325 degrees for 35 minutes, checking frequently to be sure the French-fried onions do not burn.

And we have been a real close family. Our three brothers have died and our sister has died. So it's just us."

—Donna McCabe

Chicken Spaghetti

Yield: 4 to 6 servings

1 (4- to 4½-pound) chicken
2 large onions, chopped
2 tablespoons butter
1 (20-ounce) can tomatoes
1 (4-ounce) can mushrooms,
   drained, sliced
Salt and pepper to taste
1 pound spaghetti
1 cup shredded sharp Cheddar
   cheese

Rinse the chicken. Combine the chicken with enough water to cover in a saucepan. Cook until tender; drain, reserving the broth in the saucepan. Remove the chicken from the bones in fairly large pieces; discard the bones and skin. Return the chicken to the broth in the saucepan. Sauté the onions in the butter in a small skillet; drain. Add the onions, tomatoes, mushrooms, salt and pepper to the chicken mixture. Bring to a boil; reduce heat. Simmer over medium heat until sauce is reduced. Cook the spaghetti using package directions; drain. Pour the cooked spaghetti into a 2-quart baking dish. Pour the chicken mixture over the spaghetti. Top with the Cheddar cheese. Bake at 400 degrees until heated through.

"It's amazing what you could do back then. But of course, like I say, the food didn't cost anything. I can remember going to the grocery with mother and she'd buy groceries for a week for five dollars."
—Mamie Strowd

Creamed Chicken with Fresh Mushrooms

Yield: 4 to 5 servings

1 (3-pound) chicken
1 pound fresh mushrooms, sliced
1 tablespoon butter
$1/2$ cup milk
2 tablespoons flour
$1/4$ teaspoon curry powder,
    or to taste

Rinse the chicken. Combine the chicken with enough water to cover in a saucepan. Cook until tender; drain, reserving the broth. Chop the chicken, discarding the skin and bones. Sauté the mushrooms in the butter in a large skillet; drain. Transfer the mushrooms to a small bowl. Combine the reserved broth and a mixture of the milk and flour in the skillet. Cook over medium heat until thickened, stirring constantly. Add the chicken and mushrooms. Season with the curry powder. Cook until heated through. Serve over cooked rice or Egg Bread (page 56).

"And daddy was a fine fellow, too. He used to pick up soldiers off the street and bring them home during World War II, because his three sons went into the service and he was afraid one of these young men didn't have a nice home-cooked meal."

—Donna McCabe

Creole Chicken

Yield: 6 to 8 servings

1 (10-ounce) can chopped tomatoes
$1/2$ onion, chopped
2 bay leaves
6 whole cloves
Dash of red pepper
Salt to taste
2 tablespoons melted butter
$1/4$ cup flour
1 pound chopped cooked chicken

Combine the tomatoes, onion, bay leaves, cloves, red pepper and salt in a saucepan. Bring to a boil; reduce heat. Cook over medium heat for 10 minutes; strain the mixture into a large bowl. Return the strained mixture to the saucepan. Add a mixture of the butter and flour. Cook over low heat until the sauce is smooth. Add the chicken; mix well. Cook until heated through. Discard the bay leaves before serving.

"We lived down off of West End most of our life growing up. And then we moved to Bellevue Drive, which is close to where I live right now."
—Mamie Strowd

Parmesan Chicken

Yield: 6 to 8 servings

1 cup seasoned bread crumbs
3 tablespoons grated Parmesan
  cheese
$2^{1}/2$ to 3 pounds boneless skinless
  chicken breasts
1 to 2 tablespoons melted butter

Mix the bread crumbs and Parmesan cheese in a plastic shaker bag. Rinse the chicken and pat dry. Cover the bottom of a 9x13-inch baking dish with the butter. Shake each chicken piece in the bag with the bread crumb mixture until well coated. Arrange the chicken in a baking dish. Bake at 325 degrees for 30 to 40 minutes or until chicken is cooked through.

Curried Chicken Giblets on Rice

Yield: 4 servings

1 pound chicken gizzards and livers

3 cups water

1 (10-ounce) can cream of
  mushroom soup

1 (4-ounce) can sliced mushrooms,
  drained

1 teaspoon curry powder

1 cup uncooked rice

Rinse the gizzards and livers. Combine the gizzards with the water in a saucepan. Bring to a boil; reduce heat. Cook until almost tender. Add the livers. Cook for 10 minutes longer. Transfer the gizzards and livers to a bowl, reserving the broth in the saucepan. Cut the gizzards into small pieces. Add the soup, mushrooms and curry powder to the broth; mix well. Cook until thickened slightly, stirring constantly. Add the gizzards and livers. Cook the rice using package directions. Spoon the giblet mixture over the rice on a serving plate.

"My other sisters just hated me because I liked to cook and they didn't."

—Mamie Strowd

Western Chicken

Yield: 2 to 3 servings

2 chicken breasts, split
2 teaspoons lemon juice
1 teaspoon dry onion flakes
Basil to taste
Pepper to taste
2/3 cup shredded Cheddar cheese
1/2 small avocado, chopped
4 thin tomato slices

Rinse the chicken and pat dry. Arrange the chicken in an 8x8-inch baking dish. Drizzle with the lemon juice. Sprinkle with the onion flakes. Season with the basil and pepper. Bake, covered with foil, at 350 degrees for 13 to 14 minutes or until the chicken is tender. Sprinkle 1/3 cup of the cheese and the chopped avocado over the chicken. Top with the tomato slices. Sprinkle the remaining cheese over the top. Bake, covered with foil, for 5 to 6 minutes longer. Let stand for 5 minutes before serving.

"After Thanksgiving, there's all this leftover turkey that you get tired of. You can make turkey cutlets one day, and then you have to make the sauce and let the cutlets sit up . . .

Turkey Cutlets

Yield: 2 dozen

1 small onion, chopped
1/2 cup margarine
3 tablespoons flour
4 cups milk
1 teaspoon Worcestershire sauce
1/4 tablespoon salt
1/4 tablespoon pepper
4 cups chopped cooked turkey
4 eggs, beaten
2 cups bread crumbs

Sauté the onion in the margarine in a large skillet until tender. Add the flour, milk, Worcestershire sauce, salt and pepper. Cook over low heat until thickened, stirring constantly. Remove from heat; let stand until cool. Add the turkey; mix well. Pour the mixture into an airtight container. Chill, covered, for 12 hours or longer. Scoop 1/4 cup of the mixture at a time; roll it in the bread crumbs, then in the beaten eggs, then back in the bread crumbs. Deep-fry at 375 degrees until brown on both sides. Drain on paper towels. May serve cutlets with a heated sauce combining cream of mushroom soup and mushrooms.

. . . let the cutlets sit up for a day, then the next day you roll them in egg and bread crumbs and fry them."

—Mamie Strowd

Turkey and Dressing

Yield: 25 to 30 servings

1 (18-pound) turkey
1 medium onion, chopped
3 ribs celery, chopped
2 quarts water
Poultry seasoning to taste
Pepper to taste
8 packages Cotton Pickin' Corn
    Bread Mix
8 eggs
2 large onions, chopped
6 ribs celery, chopped
1 teaspoon poultry seasoning
Salt and pepper to taste
2 tablespoons flour
1 cup water

"The first time I had to cook a turkey, I didn't know what to do with it . . . you don't know how many people have cooked a turkey and when they've gotten through, they see that bag of giblets up in the neck cavity."
—Donna McCabe

Rinse the turkey. Place the turkey in a large roasting pan. Add the chopped medium onion and chopped 3 ribs of celery. Pour the water over the top. Sprinkle the turkey with the poultry seasoning and pepper to taste. Prepare the corn bread using package directions. Crumble the corn bread into a large bowl. Add the chopped large onions, chopped 6 ribs of celery, 1 teaspoon poultry seasoning, salt and pepper to taste; mix well. Bake the turkey at 325 degrees for 2 hours; add enough turkey broth to the corn bread mixture just to moisten. Stuff the turkey with the corn bread mixture. Bake for 2 to 3 hours longer or until the turkey is tender. Remove the turkey from the roasting pan. Combine the remaining broth with the flour and 1 cup water for gravy. Cook over low heat until thickened, stirring constantly.

Patio Crab Casserole

Yield: 8 to 10 servings

2 cups chopped onions

1/4 cup butter or margarine

1 pound frozen Alaskan king crab,
  thawed

1/2 cup chopped parsley

2 tablespoons snipped chives

2 pimentos, chopped

1 1/2 cups corn muffin mix

1/8 teaspoon salt

1 egg, beaten

1/2 cup milk

1 cup cream-style corn

2 cups sour cream

1 cup shredded Cheddar cheese

Sauté the onions in the butter in a skillet until tender. Stir in the crab meat, parsley, chives and pimentos. Cook over low heat, stirring occasionally. Combine the corn muffin mix, salt, egg, milk and corn in a medium bowl, stirring just to moisten. Pour the batter into a greased 3-quart shallow baking dish, spreading the batter evenly to the edges. Spoon the crab meat mixture over the top. Spread the sour cream over the crab meat mixture. Sprinkle the Cheddar cheese over the top. Bake at 400 degrees for 25 to 30 minutes. May substitute two 7-ounce cans Alaskan king crab for the frozen crab meat.

"I've done that. Christmas morning I got ready to serve the turkey and I thought, what is this thing hanging out the end of it? It was a bag of giblets."

—Mamie Strowd

Scalloped Oysters

Yield: 4 servings

1 pint fresh oysters
4 ribs celery, chopped
1/2 pound saltine crackers, crushed
1/2 cup melted margarine
1 (6-ounce) can sweetened
   condensed milk
Salt and pepper to taste

Drain the oysters, reserving the liquid. Layer the oysters, celery, cracker crumbs and melted margarine 1/2 at a time in a nonstick baking pan. Combine the reserved oyster liquid and the condensed milk in a bowl; mix well. Pour over the layers until the baking pan is 3/4 full. Season with salt and pepper. Bake at 325 degrees for 20 to 30 minutes or until the oysters are done to taste.

"Well, the other night, we fixed this shrimp dish that my husband used to fix. My daughter and I fixed it and Donna came down to eat and she said it was delicious. But Donna thinks everything is delicious . . .

Shrimp and Crab with Almonds

Yield: 6 to 8 servings

1 cup (heaping) shrimp
1 cup (heaping) crab meat
2 (10-ounce) can cream of
   mushroom soup
1 cup finely chopped celery
1/4 cup chopped green onions
1 (3-ounce) can Chinese fried noodles
1 (2-ounce) package slivered
   toasted almonds

Combine the shrimp, crab meat, soup, celery and green onions in a bowl; mix well. Spoon into a 2-quart casserole. Chill, covered, until ready to bake. Fold in the Chinese noodles. Sprinkle the almonds over the top. Bake at 375 degrees for 25 minutes or until heated through. Serve hot.

Creole Shrimp Casserole

Yield: 6 to 8 servings

1 medium onion, chopped

1/2 to 2/3 cup chopped bell peppers

4 ribs celery, chopped

1/2 cup margarine

Salt and pepper to taste

1/4 teaspoon garlic powder

1 (6-ounce) package Uncle Ben's
    Long Grain and Wild Rice

1/2 pint whipping cream

Tabasco sauce to taste

2 (15-ounce) cans tomato sauce

1 (3-ounce) can tomato paste

2 to 3 pounds medium shrimp,
    cooked, peeled, deveined

1 pound sharp Cheddar cheese,
    shredded

Sauté the onion, bell peppers and celery in the margarine in a large skillet. Season with the salt, pepper and garlic powder. Cook the rice using package directions. Combine the whipping cream, Tabasco sauce, tomato sauce and tomato paste in a bowl; mix well. Combine the vegetable mixture, rice and the shrimp with just enough of the sauce mixture to moisten in a large bowl; mix well. Spoon into a 9x13-inch casserole. Sprinkle the cheese over the top. Bake at 350 degrees until bubbly in the center. May substitute one 12-ounce package frozen onions for the fresh onion.

This is really my husband's recipe, so when he said it was really good, it had to be, because he's very critical."
—Mamie Strowd

Red Snapper

Yield: 4 servings

4 red snapper fish
2 cups water
1/4 cup chopped celery
1/4 cup chopped onion
2 cups bread crumbs
3 (4-ounce) cans crab meat
Lemon butter to taste
2 cups white sauce or cream sauce
2 hard-cooked eggs, chopped
1 cup shrimp
1 cup sliced mushrooms

"We're always busy. You know, trying to keep up with George is a full-time job all in itself. He does a lot of catering."

—Donna McCabe

Fillet the fish, reserving the bones. Combine the bones with the water, chopped celery and chopped onion in a small saucepan. Bring to a boil; reduce heat. Simmer over low heat until vegetables are tender; drain reserving the broth. Combine the bread crumbs and crab meat with enough of the fish broth to moisten in a bowl; mix well. Stuff the crab meat mixture loosely inside the filleted fish. Arrange in a baking dish. Bake at 325 degrees until tender and flaky, basting frequently with the lemon butter. Prepare the white sauce. Add the hard-cooked eggs, shrimp and mushrooms. Cook over low heat until heated through. Spoon over the stuffed fish before serving.

"The last Sunday I was there,
I served 836 people . . ."

—Stella Maynard,
Loveless owner 1957–1974

In the 1960s, the media began to take notice of the funky little establishment out on Highway 100. Soon it was standing room only on Saturday nights and Sunday mornings. There had been talk of expansion, of building a new place. But a new Loveless just wouldn't be the Loveless anymore, so the Maynards decided to keep it the way it was.

"People came because it reminded them of home," says Stella Maynard. "If they were traveling, or if they were on the road, they wanted a comfortable place. That's what made the Loveless what it was: the way we ran it." Like Mr. Lon and Miss Annie, Cordell and Stella divided up the chores. Cordell took care of the ham business and the outside work, and Stella did the kitchen and hotel work.

"My husband was very particular about those hams," Stella says. "He'd buy them carefully and slice them himself. Ham was the most popular dish and we knew it."

They also had good help, particularly in the kitchen. Mary Elizabeth Roberts stayed with the restaurant until the 1980s. Marie Greer waited tables for more than twenty years.

"We sold it, finally, because we were tired and worn out," says Stella. "We owned it for sixteen years and signed the last papers on Easter Sunday, 1974."

continued on page 134

VEGETABLES
& SIDE DISHES

Artichokes

Yield: 6 servings

6 artichokes
1 tablespoon salt

Cut the stems and tough bottom leaves off the artichokes; rinse. Bring 2 quarts of water to a boil; add the salt. Add the artichokes. Cook, covered, for 35 minutes or until the leaves will pull off easily. Drain the artichokes; serve with a favorite sauce.

> "You wouldn't believe how many vegetables we serve. Lots, a lot. People just like real food."
> —Donna McCabe

Artichokes and Asparagus

Yield: 6 to 8 servings

1 (14-ounce) can artichoke hearts, drained
1 (11-ounce) can asparagus spears
1/2 cup mayonnaise
1 tablespoon mustard
1/4 cup butter
Dash of red pepper
Dash of onion salt
Juice of 1/2 lemon

Rinse the artichokes in cold water; drain. Cook the artichokes and asparagus together using package directions until tender; drain. Arrange the artichokes and asparagus in a 2-quart casserole. Combine the mayonnaise, mustard, butter, red pepper and onion salt in the top of a double boiler. Cook over medium heat until blended, stirring frequently. Add the lemon juice; mix well. Pour the sauce over the cooked vegetables. Serve hot.

Asparagus Casserole

Yield: 6 servings

2 (15-ounce) cans asparagus
   spears, drained
1 (10-ounce) can Cheddar cheese
   soup
3 hard-cooked eggs

Arrange the asparagus in a 2-quart casserole. Spread the soup over the asparagus. Slice the hard-cooked eggs over the top. Bake at 350 degrees until the asparagus is tender. Serve hot.

Asparagus Supper

Yield: 10 servings

8 hard-cooked eggs
2 (15-ounce) cans asparagus spears
1 cup chopped cooked country ham
   or chipped beef
2 (10-ounce) cans cream of celery
   soup or 2 cups cream sauce
1 cup shredded Cheddar cheese

Cut each of the hard-cooked eggs into 8 pieces. Drain the asparagus, reserving 1/2 the liquid. Arrange the asparagus in a 9x13-inch buttered baking dish. Sprinkle with the hard-cooked eggs and country ham. Pour a mixture of the reserved liquid and soup evenly over the top. Sprinkle with the cheese. Bake at 375 degrees until bubbly.

"The most popular are the green beans and creamed potatoes and the shoe peg corn."
—Donna McCabe

Green Beans

Yield: 6 to 8 servings

2 pounds snap beans or pole beans
1/2 pound hog jowl
1 medium onion, chopped
Salt and pepper to taste

Break the beans into 1-inch pieces; rinse thoroughly and drain. Combine the beans, hog jowl, onion, salt and pepper, and enough water to cover in a pressure cooker; seal. Cook for 30 minutes, using manufacturer's directions. Remove the top. Reduce heat; simmer for 1 hour or until the water is absorbed. May cook beans with water and seasonings in a covered saucepan until tender, then remove cover and cook until water is absorbed.

"Most of the customers now choose two vegetables. All these long years, we served just French fries and tossed salad with the meals and then we decided we'd try vegetables. ➤

Green Bean Casserole

Yield: 6 to 8 Servings

2 (16-ounce) cans French-style
  green beans, drained
1 (10-ounce) can cream of
  mushroom soup
1 tablespoon lemon juice
1/2 teaspoon Lawry's seasoned salt
1 (3-ounce) can French-fried
  onion rings

Combine the beans, soup, lemon juice and seasoned salt in a bowl; mix well. Spoon into a 2-quart casserole. Bake at 325 degrees until bubbly. Sprinkle the French-fried onion rings over the top. Bake for 2 minutes longer.

VEGETABLES

Broccoli with Garlic Cheese

Yield: 8 to 10 servings

1 onion, chopped
2 tablespoons butter
3 (10-ounce) packages frozen
   chopped broccoli, thawed
1 (6-ounce) can mushrooms
1 (8-ounce) roll garlic cheese, cut
   into pieces
1 (10-ounce) can cream of
   mushroom soup
Dash of MSG

Sauté the onion in the butter in a large skillet. Add the broccoli. Cook over low heat until the broccoli is tender, stirring frequently. Add the mushrooms, garlic cheese, soup and MSG. Cook over low heat until the cheese melts, stirring frequently. May add a small amount of milk if the mixture is too thick.

And some people said, 'Oh, that won't work, you know.' But you wouldn't believe how many vegetables we serve."

—Donna McCabe

Broccoli with Dressing

Yield: 4 servings

1 (10-ounce) package frozen
   broccoli florets, thawed
3 tablespoons vegetable or olive oil
3 tablespoons vinegar
1 tablespoon chopped onion
2 chopped pimentos
1 hard-cooked egg, chopped
1 teaspoon salt
1 teaspoon parsley

Cook the broccoli using package directions; drain. Combine the oil, vinegar, onion, pimentos, hard-cooked egg, salt and parsley in a small saucepan; mix well. Bring to a boil; reduce heat. Pour over the broccoli before serving. May serve with asparagus.

Donna's Broccoli and Rice

Yield: 4 or 5 servings

1 small onion, chopped
1 tablespoon vegetable oil
1 (10-ounce) package chopped
    broccoli, thawed
1 (10-ounce) can cream of
    mushroom soup
1 cup shredded American cheese
1 teaspoon salt
1 1/2 cups cooked rice

Sauté the onion in the oil in a large skillet. Add the broccoli. Cook for 5 minutes over medium heat, stirring constantly. Add the soup. Bring to a boil; reduce heat, stirring frequently. Add the cheese, salt and rice; mix well. Cook until heated through. Serve hot.

"To make dry bread crumbs, cut six slices of bread into half-inch cubes. Microwave the cubes in a three-quart casserole for six or seven minutes, stirring, until they are dry. Crush the cubes in the blender."

Broccoli and Water Chestnuts Casserole

Yield: 8 servings

2 (10-ounce) packages frozen
    broccoli, thawed
2 (5-ounce) cans sliced water
    chestnuts, drained
2 (10-ounce) cans cream of chicken
    soup
1/4 cup melted butter
1/2 cup grated Parmesan cheese
1/4 cup bread crumbs

Cook the broccoli using package directions; drain. Combine the broccoli, water chestnuts, soup, butter, Parmesan cheese and bread crumbs in a large bowl; mix well. Spoon into a 2-quart casserole. Bake at 350 degrees for 1 hour or until bubbly.

Cauliflower in Cheese Sauce

Yield: 4 to 6 servings

1 large head fresh cauliflower
1/4 cup margarine or butter
1 tablespoon flour
1 cup milk
1/2 pound Velveeta cheese

Rinse the cauliflower; break into florets. Cook the cauliflower in 2 cups salted water just until tender; drain. Combine the margarine and flour in a saucepan over medium heat. Add the milk. Cook over medium heat until thickened, stirring constantly. Add the cheese, stirring frequently until the cheese is melted. Pour over the cauliflower in a serving bowl; mix gently. Serve with turkey, lamb or roast.

Corn on the Cob

Yield: 4 to 8 servings

4 to 8 ears of fresh corn
1/4 cup sugar
1 cup milk

Combine the corn with enough water to cover in a deep saucepan. Stir in the sugar and milk. Bring to a boil; reduce heat. Simmer, covered, for 20 minutes or longer.

"Well, all of it's fresh that we cook, fresh all the time. We cook our vegetables every day and we cook our meats to order. We don't have any old food sitting around."
—Donna McCabe

Fried Corn

Yield: 4 to 6 servings

6 ears Silver Queen or other
    white corn
1/2 cup bacon drippings
Salt and pepper to taste
2 cups water
1 cup milk

Cut and scrape the corn off the cobs with the milky corn liquid into a large cast-iron skillet. Add the bacon drippings, salt and pepper. Cook for 3 minutes over high heat, stirring constantly. Add the water; reduce heat. Cook over medium heat until water is absorbed, stirring frequently. Stir in the milk. Cook over low heat until the milk is absorbed, stirring occasionally. Serve immediately.

"Just when and how the tradition found its way into our heritage is not known to me, but it is the custom to eat black-eyed peas on New Year's Day if you want to have good luck in the coming year.

➥

Fried Corn with Jalapeño Peppers

Yield: 8 servings

1/3 cup bacon drippings
8 ears Silver Queen corn
1 cup water
2 teaspoons salt
3 jalapeño peppers, minced

Pour the bacon drippings into a large cast-iron skillet. Cut and scrape the corn off the cobs with the milky corn liquid into the skillet. Add the water, salt and jalapeños; mix well. Cook over medium heat for 30 minutes or until the liquid is absorbed, stirring frequently. Add more water if needed. May use more or less jalapeños.

VEGETABLES

Black-Eyed Peas

Yield: 4 servings

1 pound fresh or dried black-eyed
  peas
1 quart water
1/2 pound hog jowl
Dash of garlic salt
Black pepper to taste
Crushed red pepper to taste

Combine the black-eyed peas with the water in a saucepan. Add the hog jowl, garlic salt, black pepper and red pepper. Bring to a boil; reduce heat to medium-high. Cook for 1 hour or until the peas are tender. May need to add water.

Au Gratin Potatoes

Yield: 6 to 8 servings

6 to 8 Idaho potatoes, sliced
1/2 onion, chopped
2 tablespoons margarine or butter
2 tablespoons flour
1 cup milk
Salt and pepper to taste
1 pound Velveeta cheese, cut
  into pieces

Cook the potatoes in enough water to cover in a saucepan until tender; drain. Sauté the onion in the margarine in a large skillet; drain. Add the flour, milk, salt and pepper to the onion; mix well. Cook over medium heat until thickened, stirring constantly. Add the cheese, stirring until the cheese melts. Arrange the potatoes into a 9x13-inch casserole. Pour the cheese mixture over the top. Bake at 350 degrees until bubbly.

"Some people (my mother for one) consider black-eyed peas only half the tradition, claiming you must also serve pork ... And we have never, never, never missed our black-eyed peas and hog jowl on New Year's Day. You think we want bad luck?" —Michael Grissom, *Southern by the Grace of God*

Cheesy Potatoes

Yield: 6 servings

8 medium unpeeled new potatoes
3/4 cup shredded sharp Cheddar
    cheese
6 slices cooked bacon, crumbled
1/2 cup melted butter

Cut the potatoes into bite-size pieces. Cook in enough boiling water to cover until tender; drain. Layer the potatoes and cheese in a 2-quart casserole. Sprinkle with the bacon. Pour the butter evenly over the top. Bake at 350 degrees until the cheese is melted. Serve hot.

"That's a funny thing. These old recipes that people wrote down, they often wrote down the ingredients and then they just stopped.

Potato Pancakes

Yield: 15 to 20 servings

3 tablespoons chopped onion
2 tablespoons butter
2 cups mashed cooked potatoes
2 eggs, beaten
1/2 cup flour
Salt and pepper to taste

Sauté the onion in the butter in a small skillet, stirring until the onion is tender; drain. Combine the potatoes, eggs, flour and onion in a small bowl; mix well. Season with salt and pepper. Drop the mixture by tablespoonfuls onto a lightly oiled griddle; press flat with a spatula. Cook until brown on both sides. Serve immediately.

Scalloped Hash Brown Potatoes

Yield: 10 servings

2 pounds frozen hash brown
 potatoes, thawed
1 (10-ounce) can cream of
 chicken soup
2 cups sour cream
1 teaspoon melted butter
1/4 teaspoon pepper
1/2 cup chopped onion
1 cup shredded sharp Cheddar
 cheese
1 cup shredded American cheese
2 cups corn flakes
1/2 cup melted butter or
 margarine

Spread the hash brown potatoes evenly in a 9x13-inch buttered baking dish. Combine the soup, sour cream, 1 teaspoon melted butter, pepper, onion and shredded cheeses in a medium bowl; mix well. Pour over the hash brown potatoes. Sprinkle a mixture of the corn flakes and 1/2 cup melted butter over the top. Bake at 350 degrees for 45 minutes. May be prepared the day before and refrigerated until baking time. May be frozen.

That's taken us a long time as we've collected these recipes, deciding how do we put this together and what temperature do we cook it at and how long do we cook it . . ."
—Donna McCabe

Creamy Squash Casserole

Yield: 6 to 8 servings

1 medium onion, chopped

1/2 clove of garlic, minced

2 tablespoons butter

1 pound fresh squash, sliced, cooked, drained

1 (10-ounce) can cream of mushroom soup

2 cups seasoned bread crumbs

1 cup sour cream

2 cups shredded Cheddar cheese

Sauté the onion and garlic in the butter in a small skillet until tender; drain. Combine the onion, garlic, cooked squash and soup in a bowl; mix well. Sprinkle 1/2 cup of the bread crumbs in the bottom of a 2-quart casserole. Layer the squash mixture, sour cream and Cheddar cheese over the bread crumbs. Sprinkle the remaining bread crumbs over the top. Bake at 350 degrees until heated through.

"Inside there's paneling on the walls, red checkered tablecloths on every table and the smell of good Southern cooking."
—Sue Chastain, *The Philadelphia Inquirer*, March 1986

Squash Casserole

Yield: 6 to 8 servings

8 to 10 fresh yellow squash
1 medium onion, chopped
1^1/$_2$ cups water
^{1}/$_4$ teaspoon salt
Dash of pepper
1 cup shredded Velveeta cheese
1 cup cracker crumbs

Rinse the squash; cut off the ends. Slice the squash into 1-inch pieces. Combine the squash and onion in a saucepan with the water. Sprinkle with the salt and pepper. Cook over medium heat until the vegetables are tender, stirring frequently; drain. Spoon into a 2-quart casserole. Stir in the Velveeta cheese. Sprinkle the cracker crumbs over the top. Bake at 350 degrees for 15 to 20 minutes or until bubbly.

"Lines and country-star sightings are both common, particularly on Sunday mornings."
—March Egerton, *Dallas Morning News*, Nov. 29, 1992

Squash in Cream

Yield: 6 to 8 servings

2 pounds fresh yellow squash

1 1/2 cups water

2 small onions, chopped

3 tablespoons butter

1 teaspoon salt

Pepper to taste

1/2 teaspoon Worcestershire sauce

1 teaspoon sugar

1 (2-ounce) jar chopped pimentos, drained

1/2 cup whipping cream

5 tablespoons grated Parmesan cheese

Rinse the squash; cut off the ends. Slice the squash into 1-inch pieces. Cook the squash in the water in a saucepan over medium heat until tender; drain. Sauté the onions in the butter in a small skillet; drain. Combine the squash, onions, salt, pepper, Worcestershire sauce, sugar, pimentos and whipping cream in a bowl; mix well. Spoon into a greased 2-quart casserole. Sprinkle the Parmesan cheese over the top. Bake at 325 degrees until bubbly.

"Donna didn't like to cook when she got married. She just plain didn't like to cook and I did."

—Mamie Strowd

Sweet Potato Casserole

Yield: 6 to 8 servings

2 (17-ounce) cans sweet potatoes,
  drained, mashed
1 (8-ounce) can crushed pineapple
1/2 (6-ounce) can orange juice
  concentrate
1/2 cup packed brown sugar
1 cup marshmallows

Combine the sweet potatoes, undrained pineapple, undiluted orange juice concentrate and brown sugar in a medium bowl; mix well. Spoon into a greased 2-quart casserole. Bake at 350 degrees for 20 minutes. Spread the marshmallows over the top. Bake for 2 minutes longer or until the marshmallows are brown.

"My daughter told me not long ago, 'I can remember when we were growing up, none of the other mothers on the street cooked, but you always had a good meal every night.'"
—Mamie Strowd

Fried Green Tomatoes

Yield: 5 to 6 servings

1 firm green tomato
1/2 cup cornmeal
Salt and pepper to taste
Vegetable oil

Rinse the tomato; cut into thick 1/8-inch slices. Dip the slices into the cornmeal, coating both sides. Pour enough oil in a skillet to measure 1/2 inch deep; heat the oil. Place the coated tomatoes in the hot oil. Brown on both sides; serve immediately.

"I try to tell them to cut the tomatoes thinner . . . they think, you know, everybody wants a big old thick piece of tomato, and you can't get it into your mouth."

—Donna McCabe

Turnip Greens

Yield: 4 to 6 servings

4 pounds fresh turnip greens
1/4 pound country ham pieces
1/4 teaspoon salt
Dash of black pepper
Dash of crushed red pepper

Remove and discard tough stems and discolored leaves from the turnip greens. Rinse the turnip greens at least 4 times; drain. Place the turnip greens in a large saucepan. Fill the saucepan 1/4 full with water. Add the country ham, salt, black pepper and red pepper. Bring to a boil; reduce heat. Cook over medium heat for about 2 hours or until the turnip greens are tender and most of the water is absorbed. Serve hot.

Vegetable Casserole

Yield: 8 to 10 servings

3 cups drained cooked fresh
   green beans
2 cups chopped green bell peppers
6 tomatoes, chopped
3 cups shredded Cheddar cheese
1 cup baking mix
1 cup milk
6 eggs
1 teaspoon salt
1/8 teaspoon cayenne pepper

Layer the green beans, green peppers, tomatoes and cheese in a 9x13-inch baking dish. Combine the baking mix, milk, eggs, salt and cayenne pepper in a small mixing bowl; mix well. Pour over the bean mixture. Bake at 350 degrees for 40 to 50 minutes. May add cooked peeled zucchini half-slices and sliced onion over the beans. May add fresh parsley. May season the baking mix with basil or tarragon.

"I eat more salt than most people, but I always add just a touch of salt when I eat black-eyed peas."

—Donna McCabe

Triple Green Vegetable Dish

Yield: 6 to 8 servings

1 (10-ounce) package frozen green
    peas, thawed
1 (10-ounce) package frozen lima
    beans, thawed
1 (16-ounce) can French-style green
    beans, drained
1 (8-ounce) can water chestnuts,
    drained
1 cup mayonnaise
1 medium onion, chopped, sautéed
1 teaspoon Worcestershire sauce
3 tablespoons melted butter
Dash of Tabasco sauce
Dash of mustard
3 hard-cooked eggs

Cook the green peas and lima beans separately, using package directions; drain. Combine the green peas, lima beans, green beans and water chestnuts in a large bowl; mix well. Combine the mayonnaise, onion, Worcestershire sauce, melted butter, Tabasco sauce and mustard in a small saucepan. Cook over low heat until blended. Spoon the bean mixture into a 2-quart dish. Spread the mayonnaise mixture evenly over the top. Grate the hard-cooked eggs over the top.

"The way my mother-in-law collected recipes is that one of her friends would serve something to her and she'd say, 'I like that—will you write the recipe down for me?' She never used recipes from a cookbook."
—Donna McCabe

Cream or White Sauce

Yield: 1 cup

2 tablespoons flour
2 tablespoons melted butter or
    margarine
1 cup milk
Salt to taste
Pepper to taste
Dash of cayenne pepper

Dissolve the flour in the melted butter in a saucepan. Add the milk, salt, pepper and cayenne pepper. Cook over low heat until thickened, stirring constantly. May add cheese.

Hollandaise Sauce

Yield: 2 cups

2 tablespoons lemon juice
1/4 cup water
Dash of red pepper
1/2 teaspoon salt
6 egg yolks, beaten
2 tablespoons butter
1 1/2 cups melted butter

Combine the lemon juice, water, red pepper and salt in a saucepan. Bring to a boil; reduce heat. Cook for 5 minutes or until liquid is reduced to 1/4 cup, stirring constantly. Add the egg yolks and 2 tablespoons butter; mix well. Add the 1 1/2 cups melted butter very gradually to the mixture in the saucepan over low heat, beating constantly. If the mixture curdles, beat in a small amount of hot water and lemon juice.

"Some of the recipes my aunt gave me have a check by them to tell me they are good . . ."
—Mamie Strowd

Cabbage Relish

Yield: variable

1 gallon green tomatoes
1 large head cabbage
6 sour pickles
1 bunch celery
6 onions
3 green bell peppers
1 teaspoon white mustard seeds
$1/2$ teaspoon cloves
$1/2$ teaspoon turmeric
3 tablespoons salt
$2^1/2$ pounds sugar
3 quarts vinegar

Process the tomatoes, cabbage, pickles, celery, onions and green peppers in a food processor until finely chopped. Pour the cabbage mixture into a saucepan. Add the mustard seeds, cloves, turmeric, salt, sugar and vinegar; mix well. Bring to a boil; reduce heat. Cook for 30 minutes over medium-high heat, stirring frequently. Ladle into hot sterilized jars, leaving $1/2$ inch headspace; seal with 2-piece lids. Process in a boiling water bath for 10 minutes.

"Now, we are all for saving money— after all, the more you save, the more you have for the other things you need, especially when you are raising a family.

Chili Sauce

Yield: variable

18 tomatoes

6 small onions

1 hot red pepper

1 cup sugar

2¹/₂ cups vinegar

2 teaspoons salt

1 teaspoon cloves

2 cinnamon sticks

1 teaspoon whole allspice

Process the tomatoes, onions and red pepper in a food processor until finely chopped. Pour into a saucepan. Add the sugar, vinegar and salt; mix well. Bring to a boil; reduce heat. Cook over medium heat for 30 to 45 minutes. Tie the cloves, cinnamon sticks and allspice in a cheesecloth bag. Place the cheesecloth bag in the vegetable mixture. Cook for 45 minutes longer or until thickened, stirring frequently. Ladle into hot sterilized jars, leaving ¹/₂ inch headspace; seal with 2-piece lids. Process in a boiling water bath for 10 minutes.

But when it comes to food, you really need to go ahead and spend what it takes to get the best quality."
—Donna McCabe

Chowchow

Yield: 8¹/₂ pints

1 head cauliflower
1 quart button onions
1 quart cucumbers
2 quarts green tomatoes
5 red bell peppers
¹/₂ cup salt
¹/₂ gallon water
1 cup flour
2 cups sugar
6 tablespoons dry mustard
1 tablespoon (heaping) celery seeds
1 tablespoon (level) turmeric
1 quart plus ¹/₂ cup vinegar

"We have a chowchow pickle we make. We do this together. It's a really good recipe my grandmother had.

Chop the cauliflower, onions, cucumbers, tomatoes and red peppers in a food processor. Place the chopped vegetables in a crock. Cover with a brine of the salt dissolved in the water. Let stand for 24 hours. Pour into a large saucepan. Cook over medium-high heat until vegetables are tender; drain. Combine the flour, sugar, dry mustard, celery seeds and turmeric in a 2-quart jar. Add enough vinegar to measure 2 quarts. Pour into a saucepan. Bring to a boil; reduce heat. Cook over medium heat until thickened, stirring frequently. Add the cauliflower mixture; mix well. Bring to a boil; remove from heat. Ladle into hot sterilized jars, leaving a ¹/₂ inch headspace; seal with 2-piece lids. Process in a boiling water bath for 10 minutes.

Spiced Cranberry Sauce

Yield: 3¹/₂ cups

1 cup water
1¹/₄ cups packed brown sugar
³/₄ cup sugar
¹/₂ cup vinegar
2 teaspoons whole cloves
2 cinnamon sticks
4 cups fresh cranberries

Combine the water, brown sugar, sugar, vinegar, cloves and cinnamon sticks in a saucepan. Bring to a boil; reduce heat. Simmer for 5 minutes. Remove the cloves and cinnamon sticks. Add the cranberries. Simmer for 5 minutes longer or until the cranberries burst open. Remove from heat; let stand until cool.

Chowchow pickle takes two days to fix and you can fix it only at certain times of the year, when you can get the ingredients."

—Donna McCabe

Corn Bread Dressing

Yield: 10 to 12 servings

1/2 large skillet of corn bread
10 biscuits
5 ribs celery, chopped
1 large onion, chopped
2 tablespoons poultry seasoning
1 teaspoon celery seeds
1 teaspoon sage
1/2 teaspoon salt
1 teaspoon pepper
7/8 gallon chicken base

Crumble the corn bread and biscuits into a large bowl. Combine the celery and onion in enough water to cover in a saucepan. Bring to a boil; reduce heat. Cook over medium heat until the vegetables are tender; drain. Stir the celery and onion into the corn bread mixture. Add the poultry seasoning, celery seeds, sage, salt and pepper; mix well. Pour the chicken base over the top; mix well. Spoon into a large baking dish. Bake at 400 degrees until heated through. To make good corn bread, use Martha White self-rising cornmeal mix with buttermilk and bacon drippings and cook it in a cast-iron skillet.

"Some of the recipes we found are fifty or more years old. I had a little box that was jammed full of recipes and most of them sounded good.

Creole Eggs

Yield: 6 to 8 servings

6 hard-cooked eggs, quartered
1/2 small onion, chopped
1/2 green bell pepper, chopped
1 rib celery, chopped
1 tablespoon (or more) butter
1/2 teaspoon salt
1 teaspoon pepper
1 1/2 teaspoons sugar
1 teaspoon Worcestershire sauce
2 tablespoons water
1 (15-ounce) cans or
    2 (8-ounce) cans tomato sauce
1 cup thick cream sauce
1 cup buttered bread crumbs

Arrange the hard-cooked eggs in the bottom of a buttered 2-quart baking dish. Sauté the onion, green pepper and celery in the butter in a skillet. Season with the salt, pepper, sugar and Worcestershire sauce. Add the water. Cook until vegetables are tender. Add the tomato sauce. Cook over low heat until mixture is of desired thickness. Pour the cream sauce over the eggs. Pour the tomato mixture over the top. Sprinkle with the bread crumbs. Bake at 350 degrees until heated through.

But if it's something I never heard of and it doesn't say how long to cook it or at what temperature, I put it back."

—Donna McCabe

Baked Deviled Eggs with Cheese Sauce

Yield: 4 to 6 servings

6 hard-cooked eggs
1/2 teaspoon dry mustard
1 tablespoon lemon juice
1/2 teaspoon grated onion
1/4 teaspoon salt
Dash of pepper
2 teaspoons mayonnaise-type salad
    dressing
Cheese Sauce

Cut the eggs in half lengthwise. Remove the egg yolks; mash the egg yolks in a bowl. Add the dry mustard, lemon juice and onion; mix well. Season with the salt and pepper. Add the mayonnaise-type salad dressing; mix well. Mound the egg yolk mixture in the egg halves. Arrange the stuffed eggs in a baking dish. Pour the Cheese Sauce over the top. Bake at 350 degrees for 25 minutes.

Cheese Sauce

2 tablespoons butter
2 tablespoons flour
1/4 teaspoon salt
Dash of Worcestershire sauce
1 cup milk
1 cup shredded Velveeta cheese

Melt the butter in a saucepan. Add the flour, salt and Worcestershire sauce. Cook for 2 minutes over low heat, stirring constantly. Add the milk gradually. Cook until thickened, stirring frequently. Add the cheese, stirring until the cheese melts.

"The reason they didn't put the cooking temperatures in a recipe is that they cooked on a wood stove."

Eggs Florentine with Creamed Spinach

Yield: 4 servings

4 tomatoes

Salt to taste

4 teaspoons butter

4 eggs

4 teaspoons melted butter

Salt to taste

2 cups cooked fresh spinach

2 tablespoons (heaping) medium
  cream sauce

Dash of Worcestershire sauce

Dash of Tabasco sauce

1/4 cup bread crumbs

2 tablespoons butter, softened

Cut a slice off the top of each tomato. Scoop pulp into a bowl. Salt the inside of tomato shells lightly. Invert the tomato shells on a rack to drain for 30 minutes. Place 1 teaspoon butter inside each tomato shell. Arrange the tomato shells cut side up in a buttered baking dish. Bake at 400 degrees for 10 minutes. Break an egg into each tomato shell. Pour 1 teaspoon melted butter over each egg in the shells. Season lightly with salt. Bake, covered with foil, for 10 minutes or until the egg white is just set. Mix the spinach, cream sauce, Worcestershire sauce and Tabasco sauce in a saucepan. Cook over medium heat until heated through; set aside. Sprinkle 1 tablespoon bread crumbs over each egg. Dot with the softened butter. Preheat the broiler. Broil the stuffed tomatoes for 1 minute or until the crumbs are light brown and the egg whites are cooked. Serve on a bed of hot creamed spinach.

They'd cook the food until it was done. You were supposed to be a good enough cook that you would know when it was done."

—Donna McCabe

Mexican Eggs

Yield: 4 servings

1/2 cup chopped onion

1/4 cup butter

3 tablespoons flour

2 cups canned chopped tomatoes

1 teaspoon dry mustard

1 teaspoon salt

2 teaspoons Worcestershire sauce

8 hard-cooked eggs

4 slices toast

1 (3-ounce) jar dried chipped beef

Sauté the onion in the butter in a medium skillet for 5 minutes. Stir in the flour. Add the tomatoes, dry mustard, salt and Worcestershire sauce; mix well. Cook over medium heat until thickened, stirring frequently. Pour into a bowl. Chill, covered, until serving time. Reheat the tomato mixture in a saucepan until heated through. Chop the hard-cooked eggs; stir into the tomato mixture. Place 1 slice of toast on each of 4 serving plates. Spoon the heated tomato mixture onto each piece of toast. Arrange the chipped beef around the tomato mixture on each.

"In those days they didn't get the recipes out of a cookbook. They got them from their mothers, I guess. They used to pass recipes down through the years."

—Donna McCabe

Festive Stuffed Eggs

Yield: 24 servings

12 hard-cooked eggs

2 tablespoons mayonnaise

2 teaspoons sweet pickle relish with
    a small amount of pickle juice

1/8 teaspoon dry mustard

1/8 teaspoon salt

Dash of pepper

Paprika to taste

Cut each egg in half lengthwise. Remove the yolks and mash in a bowl. Add the mayonnaise, pickle relish with juice and dry mustard; mix well. Stir in the salt and pepper. Mound the mixture into each egg half. Sprinkle with the paprika. Chill, covered, until serving time.

Stuffed Eggs

Yield: 12 servings

6 hard-cooked eggs

2 tablespoons Hellman's mayonnaise

1/2 teaspoon Durkee's dressing

1 teaspoon sweet pickle relish

Cut each egg in half lengthwise. Scoop out the yolks into a bowl. Mash the yolks in the bowl. Add the mayonnaise, Durkee's dressing and pickle relish; mix well. Mound the mixture into each egg half. Chill, covered, until serving time.

"My aunt gave me some recipes that came from her mother—some really old ones that say, 'Add some butter the size of an egg.'"
—Mamie Strowd

Marinated Mushrooms

Yield: 4 to 6 servings

2 (4-ounce) cans mushroom buttons
1 cup Italian salad dressing

Stir the mushrooms into the Italian dressing in a bowl. Chill, covered, for 10 to 12 hours before serving.

"Now, I know Mamie's nervous about using measurements in recipes. Mamie just cooks by feel. She knows how much it takes."
—Donna McCabe

Sweet Pickled Peaches

Yield: variable

9 pounds whole peaches, peeled
3 pounds sugar
1 1/2 pints vinegar
Cinnamon to taste
Cloves to taste
Spices to taste

Place the peaches in a large stockpot with a mixture of the sugar and vinegar. Add the cinnamon, cloves and spices. Cook until peaches are tender enough to pierce with a straw. Remove the peaches from the syrup. Bring the syrup to a boil; reduce heat. Cook the syrup over medium heat until thickened, stirring constantly. Place the peaches back in the syrup. Spoon the peaches into hot sterilized jars. Pour the syrup over the peaches in each jar leaving 1/2 inch headspace; seal with 2-piece lids. Process in a boiling water bath for 10 minutes.

Bread and Butter Pickles

Yield: variable

6 quarts cucumbers, sliced

1 quart onions, sliced

4 large green bell peppers, finely
  chopped

1 cup salt

9 cups water

3 pounds sugar

3 pints vinegar

1 teaspoon white mustard

1 teaspoon celery seeds

*Combine the cucumbers, onions
and green peppers in a large crock.
Cover with a brine of salt dissolved
in the water. Let stand for 3 hours;
drain. Combine the sugar, vinegar,
white mustard and celery seeds in a
large saucepan. Add the cucumber
mixture; mix well. Bring just to a
boiling point; do not boil. Remove
from heat. Ladle the cucumber mixture
into hot sterilized jars, leaving a
1/2 inch headspace; seal with 2-piece
lids. Process in a boiling water bath
for 10 minutes.*

"Dump and taste."
—Mamie Strowd

Pickled Green Tomatoes

Yield: 5 pints

4 pounds green tomatoes, sliced

4 cups sugar

1/2 cup lime

1 gallon water

1 to 1 1/2 quarts vinegar

1 tablespoon (heaping) pickling
   spice

Rinse the tomatoes 4 times or more; drain. Pour a mixture of the sugar, lime and water over the tomatoes in a large container. Let stand, covered, for 8 to 10 hours. Combine the vinegar and pickling spice in a large saucepan. Cook until heated through. Add the tomato mixture. Bring to a boil; reduce heat. Cook over medium-high heat for 30 minutes. Ladle into hot sterilized jars, leaving 1/2 inch headspace; seal with 2-piece lids. Process in a boiling water bath for 10 minutes.

"I think that one of the things that people like about coming out here is that it's an event. And it may sound kind of corny . . . but there's something to what Donna said about real food, honest food."

—Mamie Strowd

"Good food, good service. If you have that, you know it's got to be good, it's got to go over. A smile, for one thing, just makes people feel welcome to come in and eat. Once they get through eating, they go out with a smile. That's what it's all about."

—*Donna McCabe, owner*

When Donna and Charlie McCabe bought the Loveless in 1974, Nashville was experiencing a dramatic change. Opryland had just opened, transforming country music from a show at a run-down gospel tabernacle into a combination Broadway musical and religious revival. The folks who ran the high-powered insurance companies, banks, and academic institutions woke up one morning and discovered that a lot of revenue was being generated from a two- or three-block strip of houses that had been converted into recording studios along 16th Avenue South. Music Row was becoming an influential area and things were hopping in Music City.

Why, when the Opry went to its new home on the banks of the Cumberland, even Richard Nixon (with the hounds of Watergate already hot on his trail) came to Music City, twirled a yo-yo with Roy Acuff, banged out a few tunes on the piano, and made national headlines. One year later, a maverick Hollywood director named Robert Altman brought a troupe of actors to town, holed up on Old Hickory Lake, and started making a movie that was all about power, politics, and the music industry. Not everybody in town liked the movie *Nashville;* Minnie Pearl, for one, said she didn't understand it, and a few others were insulted, probably because they didn't recognize themselves. But when the film was nominated for an Academy Award and movie critics pronounced themselves lovestruck over Altman's "Epic of Country Music," people begin to think it was great.

By then, of course, the Loveless had taken its rightful place as an American, and especially a Nashville, institution. Altman's actors ate at the Loveless and so did the music people. Donna and Charles McCabe caught the Loveless at just the right moment, when it was being transformed from a relic along the highway into a piece of nostalgia.

The McCabes bought the Loveless on the advice of their son, who ran the Natchez Trace Inn in Bellevue. Donna and Charlie both came from Nashville and had a history in the restaurant business. Donna Killebrew McCabe had come from a big family, a family of good cooks, and she met Charlie when she was working at his first restaurant, the Pepper Pot, in downtown Nashville. Charlie later owned the first Bonanza franchise in Nashville and went on to own several in both Tennessee and Kentucky.

"Charlie just loves the restaurant business," Donna says. "I couldn't have made him do anything else even if I had wanted to."

In 1986 the McCabes decided to close the motel part of the Loveless. Spreading, suburbanized Nashville was no longer a place of downtown hotels: the Maxwell House burned; the Hermitage closed, then reopened. The Sam Davis, James Robertson, and Andrew Jackson hotels were either torn down or turned into apartments. Out on West End and in Franklin and on the north side of town, the Holiday Inns and Hampton Inns began to sprout up—modern central-air-conditioned high rises without the character or the defects of an old, whitewashed motor inn along Highway 100.

So the motel was closed, leaving the McCabes with only the restaurant part to run. Only the restaurant! Well, shoot, what do you do when 75 people come in at one time and want to eat *now?* What do you do when they're standing outside in the afternoon heat, mouths watering for biscuits and jam? It's like Donna says: "People just like real food."

continued on page 183

DESSERTS

DESSERTS

Apple Cake

Yield: 15 servings

4 medium apples, chopped
1/2 cup sugar
1 1/2 teaspoons cinnamon
3 cups flour
2 teaspoons baking powder
1 teaspoon salt
1 teaspoon baking soda
2 cups sugar
4 eggs
1/3 cup orange juice
1 cup vegetable oil
2 teaspoons vanilla extract
Cream Cheese and Pecan Icing

Combine the apples, sugar and cinnamon in a small bowl; mix well. Combine the flour, baking powder, salt, baking soda and sugar in a large mixer bowl. Add the eggs 1 at a time, mixing well after each addition. Stir in the orange juice, oil and vanilla. Layer the batter and the apple mixture 1/2 at a time in a nonstick 9x13-inch cake pan. Bake at 350 degrees for 1 hour and 15 minutes. Spread the Cream Cheese and Pecan Icing over the cooled cake.

Cream Cheese and Pecan Icing

8 ounces cream cheese, softened
1/4 cup butter, softened
1 (1-pound) package confectioners' sugar
1/2 cup (or more) chopped pecans

Beat the cream cheese and butter in a small mixing bowl until light and fluffy. Add the confectioners' sugar; mix well. Stir in the pecans.

> "Everything I cook is fattening. That's what makes it good. I don't know how to cook anything that's not fattening."
> —Mamie Strowd

DESSERTS

Applesauce Cake

Yield: 16 servings

1 cup sugar
1/2 cup butter
1 cup applesauce
2 cups flour
1 teaspoon baking soda
1 teaspoon cloves
1 teaspoon cinnamon
1 cup chopped nuts
1/2 cup raisins

Combine the sugar, butter and applesauce in a mixer bowl; mix well. Add a mixture of the flour, baking soda, cloves and cinnamon; mix well. Stir in the nuts and raisins. Pour into a nonstick tube pan. Bake at 375 degrees for 1 hour. Invert onto a serving plate.

"Oh, I can't tell you how many calories —do I have to do that?"

—Donna McCabe

Chocolate Rum Cake

Yield: 16 servings

1/2 cup chopped pecans
1 (2-layer) package butter-recipe
    fudge cake mix
1/2 cup rum
1 cup water
1 cup vegetable oil
1 (4-ounce) package vanilla
    pudding mix
4 eggs
Rum Glaze

Sprinkle the pecans in the bottom of a greased and floured bundt pan. Combine the cake mix, rum, water, oil and pudding mix in a mixer bowl. Add the eggs 1 at a time, mixing well after each addition. Pour the batter over the pecans. Bake at 325 degrees for 50 to 60 minutes. Invert onto a serving plate. Pour the Rum Glaze over the top. Let stand for 30 minutes before serving.

Rum Glaze

1/4 cup rum
1/4 cup water
1/2 cup butter
1 cup sugar

Combine the rum, water, butter and sugar in a small saucepan. Bring to a boil; reduce heat. Cook over low heat until the sugar dissolves, stirring constantly.

"We had more compliments yesterday . . . everybody was talking about how good everything was."
—Donna McCabe

Coca-Cola Cake

Yield: 15 servings

2 cups self-rising flour
2 cups sugar
1 1/2 cups miniature marshmallows
1/2 cup margarine
1/2 cup vegetable oil
3 tablespoons baking cocoa
1 cup Coca-Cola
1/2 cup milk
2 eggs
Coca-Cola Icing

Combine the flour, sugar and marsh-mallows in a large bowl; mix well. Melt the margarine in a medium saucepan. Add the oil, cocoa and Coca-Cola; mix well. Pour into the flour mixture; mix well. Stir in the milk and eggs; mix well. Pour into a greased 9x13-inch cake pan. Bake at 350 degrees for 30 to 40 minutes. Pour the Coca-Cola Icing over the warm cake in the pan.

Coca-Cola Icing

1/2 cup margarine
3 tablespoons baking cocoa
3 tablespoons Coca-Cola
1 (1-pound) package confectioners' sugar

Melt the margarine in a small saucepan. Remove from heat. Stir in the cocoa and Coca-Cola; mix well. Add the confectioners' sugar gradually, stirring constantly.

"They like to see one of us around and we are, most of the time. And if I'm out a day, they say, 'Well you played hooky yesterday—*I was in.*'"

—Donna McCabe

Never-Fail Gingerbread with Lemon Sauce

Yield: 12 servings

$1/2$ cup melted shortening
$1/2$ cup sugar
$1/2$ cup sorghum molasses
2 cups flour
$1/2$ teaspoon salt
1 teaspoon baking soda
1 teaspoon ground ginger
1 teaspoon cinnamon
1 cup hot water
Lemon Sauce

Combine the shortening, sugar and molasses in a mixer bowl; mix well. Add a sifted mixture of the flour, salt, baking soda, ginger and cinnamon alternately with the hot water, mixing well after each addition. Pour into a nonstick 5x9-inch loaf pan. Bake at 350 degrees for 45 minutes. Remove to a wire rack to cool. Spoon the Lemon Sauce over individual slices.

Lemon Sauce

1 cup water
$1/2$ cup sugar
1 tablespoon cornstarch
$1/8$ teaspoon salt
2 tablespoons butter
2 tablespoons lemon juice
1 egg yolk, beaten

Bring the water to a boil in a small saucepan. Add the sugar, cornstarch and salt; reduce heat. Cook over low heat for 5 minutes, stirring frequently. Remove from heat. Add the butter, lemon juice and egg yolk; mix well. Cook over low heat for 3 minutes or until thickened, stirring constantly.

"We would go to visit my grandparents and I can remember smelling the chocolate cakes that my grandmother made . . ."
—Donna McCabe

Jam Cake

Yield: 16 servings

1 cup butter or margarine, softened

2 cups sugar

1 teaspoon baking soda

1 cup buttermilk

4 egg yolks, beaten

3 cups flour

2 teaspoons cinnamon

1 teaspoon nutmeg

1 teaspoon ground cloves

1 teaspoon allspice

1 teaspoon vanilla extract

1 cup blackberry jam

4 egg whites, beaten

3/4 cup (or less) chopped nuts

2 cups sugar

1 cup milk

1 cup butter

Cream 1 cup butter and 2 cups sugar in a large mixing bowl until light and fluffy. Dissolve the baking soda in the buttermilk in a small bowl. Beat in the egg yolks. Sift the flour, cinnamon, nutmeg, cloves and allspice into a medium mixing bowl. Add the egg yolk mixture gradually; mix well. Add the egg yolk mixture to the butter mixture in the large mixing bowl; mix well. Stir in the vanilla and blackberry jam. Fold in the egg whites. Stir in the nuts. Pour the mixture into a nonstick tube pan. Bake at 350 degrees for 40 minutes or until cake springs back when touched lightly in the center. Invert the cake onto a serving plate. Pierce the hot cake slightly. Combine the remaining sugar, milk and remaining butter in a small saucepan. Cook over medium heat until thickened, stirring constantly. Pour over the top of the cake. Let stand for 30 minutes before serving.

"My mother-in-law . . . had the best sweet recipes, because she loved sweets."

—Mamie Strowd

Nut and Date Cake

Yield: 12 servings

1 pound seeded dates
1 pound pecan halves
1$^1/_2$ cups sugar
1 cup flour
1 teaspoon salt
1 teaspoon baking powder
4 egg yolks
4 egg whites
$^1/_2$ teaspoon vanilla extract

Cut the dates into halves; mix with the pecan halves in a large bowl. Add the sugar; mix well. Sift the flour, salt and baking powder 3 times; add to the date mixture. Beat the egg yolks; add to the date mixture. Beat the egg whites in a small mixing bowl until stiff peaks form. Stir in the vanilla. Add to the date mixture. Pour into a nonstick cake pan. Bake at 225 degrees for 1 hour and 15 minutes. Remove to a wire rack to cool completely.

"Mamie's husband traveled and my husband traveled some, and we had five children, that's all there is to it. Because her children are just like mine and mine are just like hers, we ate together a lot. We fixed it and they ate it.

◆▸

1-2-3-4 Cake

Yield: 15 servings

1 cup butter, softened

2 cups sugar

4 egg yolks

3 cups flour

2 teaspoons (heaping) baking
   powder

Pinch of salt

1 cup milk

4 egg whites

*Beat the butter and sugar until smooth
and creamy. Beat the egg yolks; add
to the butter mixture. Sift the flour,
baking powder and salt together; add
to the butter mixture alternately with
the milk, mixing well after each addition. Beat the egg whites in a small
mixer bowl until soft peaks form. Fold
into the butter mixture. Pour into a
9x13-inch nonstick cake pan. Bake at
350 degrees for 30 to 35 minutes or
until a wooden pick inserted in the
center comes out clean.*

Well, it was a good
life . . . We were
always together.
We have five
children—I have
three and she has
two, but we
have five."
—Donna McCabe

Pineapple Upside-Down Cake

Yield: 8 to 10 servings

$^1/_2$ cup butter
1 cup packed brown sugar
1 (8-ounce) can pineapple slices
8 to 10 maraschino cherries
1 cup flour
1 cup sugar
1 teaspoon baking powder
3 egg yolks
3 egg whites
Whipped cream

"A lot of our customers brought their babies out here, you know, their first trip out of the hospital. Now they're grown and married and bring *their* babies out here for the first time."

—Donna McCabe

Melt the butter in an ovenproof cast-iron skillet. Stir in the brown sugar. Drain the pineapple, reserving 5 table-spoons of the juice. Arrange the pineapple slices over the brown sugar mixture. Place a maraschino cherry in the center of each pineapple slice. Combine the flour, sugar and baking powder in a medium mixing bowl. Add the egg yolks and the reserved pineapple juice; mix well. Beat the egg whites in a small mixing bowl; fold into the egg yolk mixture. Pour the mixture over the pineapple slices in the skillet. Bake at 350 degrees for 30 to 35 minutes. Invert immediately onto a serving plate. Top each serving with a dollop of whipped cream.

DESSERTS

Piña Colada Cake

Yield: 16 servings

1 (2-layer) package yellow cake mix
1 (8-ounce) can Coco Lopez
3/4 cup 80-proof rum
4 eggs
1/2 cup butter, softened
1 (8-ounce) can crushed pineapple
1 (7-ounce) package grated coconut

Pour the dry cake mix into a large mixing bowl. Add a mixture of the Coco Lopez and rum; mix well. Fold in the eggs 1 at a time, mixing well after each addition. Add the butter, pineapple and coconut, mixing well after each addition. Pour into a nonstick bundt pan. Bake at 350 degrees for 30 to 35 minutes or until a wooden pick inserted in the center comes out clean. Let cool in the pan for 15 minutes. Invert onto a serving plate.

Jean's Pound Cake

Yield: 16 servings

2 cups sugar
2 cups flour
Dash of salt
1 cup margarine, softened
5 eggs
1 teaspoon vanilla extract

Combine the sugar, flour, salt, margarine and eggs in a mixer bowl; mix well. Stir in the vanilla. Pour into a nonstick tube pan. Bake at 325 degrees for 1 hour. Invert onto a serving plate. May substitute lemon or orange flavoring for the vanilla.

"I'll tell them that I've got a table if they don't mind sitting together. It's up to them whether they want to or not . . . if they do, when they leave they say, that was fun, we met some interesting people . . ."

—Donna McCabe

Swedish Cakes

Yield: 48 servings

1 cup butter, softened
2 cups sugar
4 eggs
3 cups sifted flour
1 teaspoon baking soda
2 teaspoons cream of tartar
1/2 cup milk
1 teaspoon vinegar
1 1/2 teaspoons vanilla extract
Bourbon Pecan Frosting
2 cups ground pecans

"Customers bring their children, you know, little babies, big children, whole families. We see the same families over and over again with their children."
—Donna McCabe

Cream the butter and sugar in a mixer bowl until light and fluffy. Add the eggs 1 at a time, mixing well after each addition. Add a mixture of the flour, baking soda and cream of tartar alternately with a mixture of the milk and vinegar, mixing well after each addition. Stir in the vanilla. Pour onto a 9x13-inch cake pan lined with waxed paper. Bake at 250 to 275 degrees for 1 hour or until done. Invert onto wire rack to cool. Wrap with a clean linen towel. Let stand for 24 hours. Remove the towel. Cut into small squares. Cover each individual square with the Bourbon Pecan Frosting. Roll the frosted cakes in the ground pecans.

Bourbon Pecan Frosting

2 cups butter
4 cups confectioners' sugar
1/2 cup bourbon
1 pound pecans, ground

Beat the butter and confectioners' sugar together in a mixer bowl until creamy. Add the bourbon; mix well. Stir in the ground pecans.

DESSERTS

Sweet Potato Cake

Yield: 16 servings

3 cups sifted flour

2 cups sugar

2 teaspoons baking powder

1/4 teaspoon salt

2 teaspoons cinnamon

1 cup vegetable oil

1 (15-ounce) can crushed pineapple

2 teaspoons vanilla extract

3 eggs

2 cups grated sweet potatoes

1 cup chopped pecans

Combine the sifted flour, sugar, baking powder, salt and cinnamon in a large mixer bowl. Add the oil, pineapple and vanilla; mix well. Add the eggs 1 at a time, mixing well after each addition. Stir in the sweet potatoes and pecans. Pour into a greased bundt pan. Bake at 350 degrees for 1 1/4 hours. Invert onto a serving plate.

"We love our customers. Sometimes though, I get so busy seating everybody and setting the table that I don't know who's here!"
—Donna McCabe (*Tennessean* interview, Feb. 9, 1994)

White Cake

Yield: 12 to 16 servings

1³/4 cups sugar
³/4 cup shortening
3 cups flour
2 teaspoons baking powder
1 cup milk
6 egg whites, beaten
3 teaspoons vanilla extract

Beat the sugar and shortening in a mixer bowl until light and fluffy. Sift the flour and baking powder together 3 times. Add the flour mixture to the sugar mixture alternately with the milk, mixing well after each addition. Fold in the beaten egg whites. Stir in the vanilla. Pour into 3 nonstick 9-inch round cake pans. Bake at 375 to 400 degrees for 30 to 40 minutes. Spread the White Icing between the layers and over the top and side of the cake.

> "Paul McCartney, at that time, he was the most famous that had ever come in. He was one of the first of the famous people that came in."
> —Donna McCabe

White Icing

3 cups sugar
1 cup water
3 egg whites
Pinch of cream of tartar

Combine the sugar and water in a saucepan. Bring to a boil; reduce heat. Cook over low heat until you can dip a wire ring into the mixture and blow a bubble; do not stir. Beat the egg whites and cream of tartar in a mixer bowl until stiff peaks form. Add the egg white mixture to the sugar mixture gradually, mixing constantly. Beat until of a creamy consistency.

DESSERTS

Never-Fail Caramel Frosting

Yield: 1 recipe

2 cups packed brown sugar

1 cup sugar

2 tablespoons light corn syrup

2 tablespoons butter

2/3 cup cream

Combine the brown sugar, sugar, corn syrup, butter and cream in a saucepan. Cook over low heat until the sugar is dissolved, stirring constantly. Cover the saucepan for 2 to 3 minutes to dissolve the sugar crystals. Cook, uncovered, over medium heat to 238 degrees on a candy thermometer, softball stage. Cool to lukewarm. Beat until the mixture is of spreading consistency.

Bourbon Candy

Yield: 3 dozen

3/4 cup broken pecans

3 tablespoons bourbon

1/2 cup margarine

1 (1-pound) package confectioners' sugar

5 blocks semisweet chocolate

1/3 block paraffin

Mix the pecans and bourbon in a small airtight container. Let stand, covered, for 8 to 10 hours. Beat the margarine and confectioners' sugar in mixer bowl until light and fluffy. Stir in the pecans. Shape by teaspoonfuls into balls. Chill, covered, for 4 to 6 hours. Melt the chocolate and paraffin in a small saucepan. Spear the balls with a wooden pick. Dip into the chocolate mixture. Let stand on waxed paper until set.

"Michael McDonald comes in all the time. I asked him to bring me a picture, an autographed picture, and he brought me one signed by all the Doobies."

—George McCabe

Candy Sea Foam

Yield: 2 dozen

2 cups packed brown sugar

1/2 cup water

1 egg white

1/2 cup chopped nuts

1 teaspoon vanilla extract

Bring the brown sugar and water to a boil in a saucepan; reduce heat. Cook over medium heat until a small amount dropped in cold water forms a ball. Beat the egg white in a mixer bowl. Beat in the brown sugar mixture. Stir in the nuts and vanilla. Beat until thickened. Drop by tablespoonfuls onto waxed paper. Let stand until set.

"Mamie and I've said the same thing at the same time, just right together come out and say the same thing. It's really amazing.

DESSERTS

Caramel Candy

Yield: 2 to 3 dozen

3 cups sugar
2 tablespoons butter or margarine
1 cup milk

Combine 1 cup of the sugar and the butter in a small skillet. Cook over low heat, stirring constantly. Add the remaining sugar to the milk in a saucepan. Cook over low heat until the sugar is completely dissolved. Stir in the butter mixture. Cook, uncovered, over medium heat to 234 to 240 degrees on a candy thermometer, soft-ball stage, stirring constantly. Remove from heat. Pour into a mixer bowl; do not scrape the bottom or side of the pan. Beat until creamy. Pour into a buttered pan. Cool until firm. Cut into squares.

We've always been close. We have had our fights, and it was always over the children when they were growing up. Mine were always perfect, and she thought hers were."

—Donna McCabe

Cocoa Fudge

Yield: 2 to 3 dozen

$2/3$ cup baking cocoa

3 cups sugar

$1/8$ teaspoon salt

$1^1/2$ cups milk

$4^1/2$ tablespoons butter

1 teaspoon vanilla extract

"We were born in 1931, right in the middle of the Depression, so there wasn't a lot of money in our household . . .

Combine the cocoa, sugar and salt in a saucepan; mix well. Stir in the milk. Bring to boil; reduce heat, stirring frequently. Cook to 232 degrees on a candy thermometer, or until a small amount of mixture forms a soft ball when dropped in cold water. Remove from heat. Add the butter. Let cool to lukewarm. Stir in the vanilla. Beat until thickened. Pour into a buttered pan. Cool until firm. Cut into squares.

Marshmallow Fudge

Yield: 3 pounds

3/4 cup margarine
1 (7-ounce) jar marshmallow creme
3 cups sugar
1 (5-ounce) can evaporated milk
2 cups chocolate chips
1 teaspoon vanilla extract
1 cup chopped nuts

Combine the margarine, marshmallow creme, sugar and evaporated milk in a saucepan. Bring to a full rolling boil; reduce heat, stirring constantly. Cook over medium heat until 234 degrees on a candy thermometer, stirring constantly. Remove from the heat. Add the chocolate chips, stirring until the chips melt. Stir in the vanilla and nuts. Pour into a buttered 9x13-inch pan. Cool until firm. Cut into squares. May omit the nuts.

. . . but there sure was a lot of love."
—Donna McCabe

Caramel Fudge Squares

Yield: 18 servings

1 (1-pound) package brown sugar
1 cup margarine
1/2 cup sugar
2 cups flour
1 teaspoon baking powder
4 egg yolks, beaten
2 cups chopped pecans
4 egg whites, beaten
1/2 cup sifted confectioners' sugar

Melt the brown sugar with the margarine in a large saucepan over low heat, stirring constantly. Add the sugar; stir until melted. Remove from heat. Add a mixture of the flour and baking powder alternately with the egg yolks, mixing well after each addition. Stir in the pecans. Fold in the egg whites. Pour into a greased 9x13-inch baking pan. Bake at 350 degrees for 40 to 45 minutes. Let stand until cool. Cut into squares. Dip each square in the confectioners' sugar to coat. May omit the pecans.

"If we needed something from the grocery store, we would skate to the store to get it."
—Mamie Strowd

DESSERTS

Chess Squares

Yield: 16 servings

6 tablespoons butter, softened

1/3 cup confectioners' sugar

1/2 cup flour

1/2 cup butter, softened

1 1/2 cups sugar

1 tablespoon yellow cornmeal

1 tablespoon vanilla extract

1 tablespoon white vinegar

3 eggs

Beat the 6 tablespoons butter in a mixer bowl until light and fluffy. Stir in the confectioners' sugar and flour; mixture will be crumbly. Press the mixture into the bottom of a 9-inch square baking pan. Bake at 350 degrees for 20 minutes or until light brown. Combine the 1/2 cup butter and sugar in a mixer bowl until light and fluffy. Stir in the cornmeal, vanilla and vinegar. Add the eggs 1 at a time, mixing well after each addition. Pour over the baked layer. Bake for 20 to 25 minutes or until filling is almost set. Let stand until cool. Cut into squares.

"My daughter makes chess squares . . . she has a lot of good recipes."
—Donna McCabe

Date Nut Bars

Yield: 16 servings

1/2 cup flour
1 teaspoon baking powder
Pinch of salt
2 eggs, beaten
1 teaspoon vanilla extract
1 cup chopped dates
1 cup chopped nuts
1/2 cup sifted confectioners' sugar

Combine the flour, baking powder and salt in a mixer bowl. Add the eggs 1 at a time, mixing well after each addition. Stir in the vanilla, dates and nuts. Pour into an nonstick square baking pan. Bake at 350 degrees for 35 minutes. Cut into squares when warm. Roll in the confectioners' sugar.

"Chet Atkins comes in quite a bit. He'll come on Saturday . . . he has for years."
—Donna McCabe

Fudge Squares

Yield: 16 servings

2 tablespoons melted butter
1 cup packed brown sugar
1 egg
2 (1-ounce) squares chocolate
1/3 cup milk
1/2 teaspoon vanilla extract
1 cup flour
1 teaspoon baking powder
1/4 teaspoon salt
1/2 cup chopped nuts

Beat the butter and sugar in a mixer bowl until creamy. Add the egg. Beat until light and fluffy. Melt the chocolate in the top of a double boiler; add to butter mixture. Stir in the milk and vanilla. Sift the flour, baking powder and salt into the butter mixture; mix well. Stir in the nuts. Pour into a greased baking pan. Bake at 300 to 325 degrees for 30 to 40 minutes. Cut into squares while warm.

Graham Toffee Bars

Yield: 4 dozen

12 graham crackers, separated into
    4 sections
1 cup margarine
1 cup packed light brown sugar
1 cup chopped nuts
1 block semisweet chocolate

Arrange the graham crackers in a single layer on a buttered baking sheet. Combine the margarine, brown sugar and nuts in a saucepan. Bring to a boil; reduce heat. Cook for 2 to 3 minutes over medium heat, stirring constantly. Spread over the graham crackers to the edge. Bake at 350 degrees for 12 minutes. Melt the chocolate in the top of a double boiler. Spread over the baked layer. Let stand until cool. Break into individual pieces.

" . . . the one whose autographed picture seems to get stolen most often from the wall [is] Captain Kangaroo (Bob Keeshan)."
—Joel McNally, *Milwaukee Journal,* Oct. 19, 1994

Turtle Squares

Yield: 18 servings

1 (2-layer) package German chocolate
    cake mix
1 (16-ounce) package caramels
1/2 cup butter
1 (6-ounce) can evaporated milk
2 cups chocolate chips

Prepare the cake mix batter using package directions. Pour half of the batter into a nonstick 9x13-inch baking pan. Bake at 350 degrees for 15 minutes. Combine the caramels, butter and evaporated milk in a saucepan. Cook over low heat until thick and creamy, stirring constantly. Pour over the baked layer. Sprinkle with the chocolate chips. Pour the remaining cake batter over the top. Bake for 20 minutes longer. Let stand until cool. Cut into squares.

"When Jane and Michael Stern came to Nashville, they'd ridden around looking and they couldn't find anything and asked a cab driver.

Almond Meringues

Yield: 2 to 3 dozen

6 egg whites
1 1/2 cups sugar
1/2 teaspoon cream of tartar
1/2 teaspoon salt
1/8 teaspoon almond flavoring

Beat the egg whites in a mixer bowl until soft peaks form. Add the sugar and cream of tartar gradually, beating until stiff peaks form. Stir in the salt and almond flavoring. Drop by spoonfuls onto a buttered baking sheet. Bake at 450 degrees until done. Let stand until cool.

DESSERTS

Butter Cookies

Yield: 3 dozen

1 cup margarine, softened
1 1/2 cups sugar
1 egg
1 teaspoon vanilla extract
2 1/2 cups flour
1 teaspoon cream of tartar
2 teaspoons baking soda
1/4 teaspoon salt

Combine the margarine and sugar in a mixer bowl until light and fluffy. Stir in the egg and vanilla. Add a mixture of the flour, cream of tartar, baking soda and salt; mix well. Drop by teaspoonfuls onto a buttered cookie sheet. Bake at 375 degrees for 10 minutes. Remove to a wire rack to cool.

Butterscotch Chip Cookies

Yield: 3 dozen

1/2 cup butter, softened
1 cup packed brown sugar
1 egg
2 cups baking mix
1/2 cup chopped pecans
1 cup butterscotch chips

Combine the butter, brown sugar, egg and baking mix in a mixer bowl; mix well. Stir in the pecans and butterscotch chips. Drop by teaspoonfuls 2 inches apart on an ungreased cookie sheet. Bake at 375 degrees for 10 minutes or until light brown.

They said, where would you go to eat if you were an out-of-towner? So he brought them out here and they fell in love with it. We stay in contact with them. They'll call up sometimes."

—Donna McCabe

DESSERTS

Brandy Cookies

Yield: 3 to 4 dozen

1 cup butter
1 1/2 cups sugar
2 eggs
1 tablespoon brandy
2 teaspoons vanilla extract
3 1/2 cups sifted flour
1/4 teaspoon salt
1/4 teaspoon cinnamon
1/4 teaspoon nutmeg

Cream the butter, sugar and eggs in a mixer bowl. Add the brandy and vanilla. Beat until fluffy. Add a sifted mixture of the flour, salt, cinnamon and nutmeg; mix well. Shape into a log. Chill, covered, for 8 to 10 hours. Roll 1/4 inch thick on a lightly floured surface. Cut with a cookie cutter. Arrange on a nonstick cookie sheet. Bake at 375 degrees for 8 minutes or until brown.

Mary Anne Cookies

Yield: 3 dozen

1 cup margarine, softened
6 tablespoons confectioners' sugar
1 to 1 1/2 teaspoons vanilla extract or lemon flavoring
2 cups flour
Nut halves, jelly or preserves
Additional confectioners' sugar

Cream the margarine, confectioners' sugar and vanilla in a mixer bowl until light and fluffy. Add the flour; mix well. Shape into small balls. Press flat on a nonstick cookie sheet. Make an indentation in each cookie with the back of a spoon. Fill the indentations with a nut half, jelly or preserves. Bake at 350 degrees for 15 to 20 minutes or until light brown. Sprinkle with additional confectioners' sugar.

"They come from England, France, everywhere. We get a lot of people from California. An unbelievable amount of people from California."
—Donna McCabe

DESSERTS

Date Nut Cookies

Yield: 3 dozen

1 cup butter

1 1/2 cups sugar

3 eggs, beaten

1/2 cup water

3 cups flour

1 teaspoon baking soda

2 teaspoons cinnamon

1/2 teaspoon allspice

1 teaspoon ground cloves

1/4 teaspoon salt

2 to 3 pounds dates, cut into
   small pieces

1 pound pecans, broken into
   small pieces

Combine the butter and sugar in a mixer bowl until light and fluffy. Add the beaten eggs and water; mix well. Add a mixture of the flour, baking soda, cinnamon, allspice, cloves and salt; mix well. Stir in the dates and pecans. Drop by spoonfuls onto an ungreased cookie sheet. Bake at 350 degrees for 15 minutes or until brown.

"That's what I was going to say. I worked in the catalog department during Christmas and we had lots of packages going to California."

—Mamie Strowd

Fruit Cookies

Yield: 215 servings

1 pound shortening
1 (1-pound) package light brown
    sugar
3 tablespoons milk
1 teaspoon vanilla extract
3 eggs
3 cups sifted flour
8 ounces red or green candied
    pineapple, cut into small pieces
1 (1-pound) package white raisins
1 cup chopped walnuts
1 teaspoon baking soda

Cream the shortening and brown sugar in a large mixer bowl until light and fluffy. Add the milk and vanilla; mix well. Add the eggs 1 at a time, mixing well after each addition. Mix 2 cups of the sifted flour with the candied pineapple, raisins and walnuts in a small bowl. Add the remaining flour and baking soda; mix well. Stir into the brown sugar mixture. Drop by small teaspoonfuls 1 inch apart on an ungreased cookie sheet. Bake at 300 degrees until light brown. Remove from the pan immediately. Let cool on parchment paper. Store in an airtight container.

"Michael Douglas was here one day sitting right in front of me. Everybody was all excited, but I said, 'Now, what are you all talking about?'"
—Donna McCabe
(*Milwaukee Journal* interview, Oct. 19, 1994)

DESSERTS

Snickerdoodles

Yield: 3 dozen

1/2 cup shortening
1 1/2 cups sugar
2 eggs
2 3/4 cups sifted flour
2 teaspoons cream of tartar
1 teaspoon baking soda
1/4 teaspoon sugar
2 teaspoons cinnamon

Combine the shortening, 1 1/2 cups sugar and eggs in a mixer bowl; mix well. Add a mixture of the sifted flour, cream of tartar and baking soda; mix well. Shape the dough into 1-inch balls. Roll the balls in a mixture of the 1/4 teaspoon sugar and cinnamon in a bowl. Arrange the balls 2 inches apart on an ungreased cookie sheet. Bake at 400 degrees for 8 to 10 minutes or until light brown.

Sugar Cookies

Yield: 40 cookies

1/2 cup sugar
1 cup margarine, softened
1 teaspoon vanilla extract
2 eggs
2 1/2 cups flour

Cream the sugar and margarine in a mixer bowl. Add the vanilla and eggs, mixing well after each addition. Stir in the flour. Roll into a ball. Chill, covered, for 1 hour or longer. Roll out 1/4 inch thick on a lightly floured surface. Cut with 2-inch cookie cutter. Place on a nonstick cookie sheet. Bake at 375 degrees until light brown.

"When Princess Anne was over for the Royal Chase, she ate here. Her entourage wanted me to close the restaurant to our regulars, but I told them I couldn't do it. To us, one hungry customer is just the same as the other."

—Donna McCabe (*Tennessean* interview, Feb. 9, 1994)

DESSERTS

Lemon Sugar Cookies

Yield: 3 to 4 dozen

1 cup butter, softened
1 teaspoon vanilla extract
1/2 teaspoon lemon juice
1 egg
1 teaspoon salt
1 cup sugar
3 teaspoons milk
1/3 cup shortening
3 1/2 cups flour
1 teaspoon baking soda
1 teaspoon cream of tartar

Mix the butter, vanilla, lemon juice, egg, salt, sugar, milk and shortening in a mixer bowl until creamy. Sift the flour, baking soda and cream of tartar together 3 times. Add to the butter mixture; mix well. Chill, covered, for 1 hour or longer. Roll very thin on a lightly floured surface. Cut with cookie cutter. Place on a nonstick cookie sheet. Bake at 350 degrees until golden brown.

Kat's Tea Cakes

Yield: 3 dozen

1 1/2 cups sugar
1 cup shortening or butter
2 eggs
2 3/4 cups flour
1 teaspoon baking soda
2 teaspoons cream of tartar
1/2 teaspoon salt

Combine the sugar and shortening in a mixer bowl, beating until fluffy. Add the eggs 1 at a time, mixing well after each addition. Add a mixture of the flour, baking soda, cream of tartar and salt; mix well. Shape into small balls. Arrange on a cookie sheet. Press flat. Bake at 350 degrees for 10 minutes.

DESSERTS

Apple Pie

Yield: 6 servings

3 tart apples, chopped

1 recipe (2-crust) pie pastry

1 tablespoon flour

1/4 cup melted butter

1 teaspoon nutmeg

1 cup sugar

3/4 cup orange juice

Arrange the apples in a pastry-lined pie plate. Pour a mixture of the flour, butter, nutmeg, sugar and orange juice over the apples. Cut the remaining pastry into strips; arrange lattice-fashion over the pie. Bake at 450 degrees for 15 minutes. Reduce oven temperature to 300 degrees. Bake for 20 to 25 minutes longer or until the crust is brown.

And he said: 'Jimmy Buffett.' I said, 'No, you're not!' "
—Donna McCabe
(*Milwaukee Journal* interview, Oct. 19, 1994)

Caramel Pie

Yield: 6 servings

1 cup water
1 cup sugar
2 tablespoons butter
1/4 cup flour
1/8 teaspoon salt
1 1/2 cups milk
2 eggs
1 teaspoon vanilla extract
1 baked 9-inch pie shell
Whipped cream and chopped nuts

Bring the water to a boil in a saucepan. Add 1/2 cup of the sugar and the butter; mix well. Bring to a boil; reduce heat. Cook over medium-high heat for 2 minutes or until caramelized, stirring constantly. Mix the remaining sugar, flour, salt and milk in the top of a double boiler. Cook until heated through. Add the caramelized mixture. Beat the eggs in a small mixer bowl. Stir a small amount of the hot mixture into the beaten eggs; stir the eggs into the hot mixture in the double boiler. Cook over low heat until the mixture coats a spoon. Remove from heat. Stir in the vanilla. Pour into the baked pie shell. Bake at 300 degrees for 15 to 20 minutes. Top with whipped cream and chopped nuts. May use only egg yolks in pie filling and reserve egg whites to make meringue for the pie if desired.

"Minnie Pearl, she was a classic. She'd come out here quite a bit. She was just a sweet lady. She was a lady and a clown.

Old-Fashioned Chocolate Pie

Yield: 6 servings

1 cup sugar
3 tablespoons (heaping) flour
3 tablespoons (heaping) baking
   cocoa
1½ cups milk
3 egg yolks
1 teaspoon vanilla extract
1 tablespoon butter
1 baked 9-inch pie shell
3 egg whites
3 tablespoons sugar

Combine 1 cup sugar, flour and cocoa in a saucepan. Add the milk alternately with the egg yolks, mixing well after each addition. Add the vanilla and butter. Cook over medium heat until thickened, stirring constantly. Beat with a spoon until as smooth as possible. Pour into the baked pie shell. Beat the egg whites in a mixer bowl until soft peaks form. Add 3 tablespoons sugar gradually, beating until stiff peaks form. Spread over the filling, sealing to the edge. Bake at 375 degrees until the meringue is light brown. Serve at room temperature.

She's from a very fine family. In fact, I've heard her tell the story about how she went to a finishing school and then decided this was what she wanted to do. Her parents weren't real happy."
—Donna McCabe (*Milwaukee Journal* interview, Oct. 19, 1994)

DESSERTS

Chocolate Chess Pie

Yield: 6 servings

1/4 cup margarine
1 1/2 cups sugar
2 tablespoons baking cocoa
2 eggs
1 teaspoon vanilla extract
1/2 cup evaporated milk
1 unbaked 9-inch pie shell

Melt the margarine in a small saucepan. Stir in the sugar and cocoa. Remove from heat. Stir in the eggs; do not beat. Stir in the vanilla and evaporated milk. Pour into the unbaked pie shell. Bake at 400 degrees for 10 minutes. Reduce oven temperature to 350 degrees. Bake for 20 to 25 minutes longer. Let stand until cool. Chill, covered, until serving time.

Coconut Pie

Yield: 6 servings

4 egg yolks
1 cup sugar
2 tablespoons flour
2 cups milk
1 teaspoon butter
1 teaspoon vanilla extract
1 cup coconut
1 baked 9-inch pie shell
1 recipe meringue

Combine the egg yolks, sugar, flour, milk and butter in a saucepan. Bring to a boil; reduce heat. Cook over medium heat until thickened, stirring constantly. Stir in the vanilla and coconut. Pour into the baked pie shell. Spread the meringue over the filling, sealing to the edge. Bake at 350 to 375 degrees until the meringue is light brown.

"It may seem like things are really different now, but a lot of homes haven't changed. I see people bring in their children, whole families, and I see them over and over again . . .

➥

Lemon Chiffon Pie

Yield: 6 servings

4 egg yolks

3/4 cup sugar

Juice of 1 1/2 lemons

1/4 teaspoon salt

1/2 tablespoon unflavored gelatin

1/3 cup cold water

4 egg whites

1/3 cup sugar

1 cooked 9-inch pie shell

Beat the egg yolks in a mixer bowl. Add a mixture of the sugar, lemon juice and salt; mix well. Pour into a saucepan. Cook over medium heat until the mixture thickens, stirring constantly; remove from the heat. Soften the gelatin in the cold water in a small bowl; add to the lemon juice mixture. Let stand until cool. Beat the egg whites in a mixer bowl until soft peaks form. Add the sugar gradually, beating until stiff peaks form. Fold the egg white mixture into the lemon juice mixture. Pour into the pie shell. Chill, covered, until serving time.

The children will grow up knowing how to behave in a restaurant . . ."

—Donna McCabe

Lemon Icebox Pie

Yield: 6 servings

1 (15-ounce) can sweetened
    condensed milk
1/2 cup lemon juice
1 teaspoon grated lemon rind
2 eggs yolks, beaten
1 (9-inch) graham cracker pie shell
2 egg whites
3 tablespoons sugar

Combine the condensed milk, lemon juice, lemon rind and egg yolks in a mixer bowl; mix well. Pour into the graham cracker pie shell. Beat the egg whites in a small mixer bowl until soft peaks form. Add the sugar gradually, beating until stiff peaks form. Spread over the filling, sealing to the edge. Bake at 350 degrees until meringue is light brown. Chill, covered, until serving time. Serve cold.

"When Mamie and I make the same dish, each one is a little bit different. I add a couple of things she doesn't and she adds a few things I don't . . .

D E S S E R T S

Lime Pie

Yield: 6 servings

1 (3-ounce) package lime gelatin
1 cup boiling water
1 cup sugar
Juice of 2 lemons
1 (13-ounce) can evaporated milk
Vanilla Wafer Pie Shell
Whipped cream
Maraschino cherries

Dissolve the gelatin in the boiling water in a mixer bowl. Add the sugar, lemon juice and evaporated milk; mix well. Pour into the Vanilla Wafer Pie Shell. Whip the whipped cream. Spread over the filling, sealing to the edge. Decorate with the maraschino cherries.

Vanilla Wafer Pie Shell

1¹/₂ cups crushed vanilla wafers
¹/₂ cup melted butter or margarine
2 tablespoons sugar

Combine the vanilla wafer crumbs and butter in a bowl; stir lightly. Add the sugar. Press into the bottom and up the sides of a 9-inch pie plate.

I love to go eat her soup and she loves to come eat my soup. They're both wonderful."

—Donna McCabe

DESSERTS

Pecan Pie

Yield: 6 servings

3 eggs
1 cup sugar
1 cup dark corn syrup
2 tablespoons butter, softened
2 tablespoons flour
1 teaspoon to 1 tablespoon vanilla
   extract
Pinch of salt
1 cup pecan halves
1 unbaked 9-inch pie shell
14 to 16 whole pecans, shelled

Combine the egg, sugar, syrup, butter and flour in a mixer bowl; mix well. Stir in the vanilla and salt. Add the pecan halves. Pour into the pie shell. Arrange the whole pecans decoratively on top of the mixture. Bake at 425 degrees for 10 minutes. Reduce oven temperature to 350 degrees. Bake for 25 to 30 minutes longer or until the pie shell is brown. Let stand for 2 hours before serving. May omit salt.

"Mamie's children say her cooking is best and my children say mine's best. But they eat both . . ."
—Donna McCabe

Strawberry Pie

Yield: 6 servings

3 ounces cream cheese, softened
1/2 cup sugar
Juice of 1 lemon
1/2 pint whipping cream
1 baked 9-inch pie shell
1 pint whole strawberries, capped
1/2 cup melted red currant jelly

Beat the cream cheese, sugar and lemon juice in a mixer bowl until light and fluffy. Whip the whipping cream in a mixer bowl. Fold in the cream cheese mixture. Spoon into the baked pie shell. Arrange the strawberries over the top. Drizzle with the melted jelly.

"We raised some smart children . . ."
—Mamie Strowd

Stir-and-Roll Pie Crusts

Yield: 2 crusts

2 cups sifted flour
1 1/2 teaspoons salt
1/2 cup vegetable oil
1/4 cup cold milk

Combine the flour and salt in a bowl. Pour the oil and milk into a measuring cup; do not stir. Add to the flour mixture; mix well. Shape the dough into a ball. Place a piece of waxed paper on a slightly damp work surface. Place half the dough on the waxed paper. Place another piece of waxed paper over the top. Roll into a 12-inch circle. Fit into a pie plate, removing the waxed paper. Repeat with the remaining dough. Bake at 350 degrees until golden brown.

Caramel Filling

Yield: 1 cup

1/2 cup buttermilk
1/4 teaspoon baking soda
1/4 cup packed brown sugar
1 cup sugar
1/4 cup butter
1/2 tablespoon vanilla extract

Combine the buttermilk, baking soda, brown sugar, sugar and butter in a saucepan. Cook over medium heat until the mixture forms a soft ball. Let stand until cool. Stir in the vanilla. Pour into a mixer bowl. Beat until creamy.

"The sign people would love for us to change that sign because it's always getting broken. ↦

Chocolate Soufflé

Yield: 6 to 8 servings

2 tablespoons butter
2 tablespoons flour
1 1/2 (1-ounce) squares chocolate
2 tablespoons hot water
3/4 cup milk
2 egg yolks, beaten
2 egg whites
Whipped cream

Melt the butter in a saucepan. Add the flour, stirring until well blended. Dissolve the chocolate in the hot water in a small bowl; add to the butter mixture. Stir in the milk. Remove from the heat. Add the egg yolks; mix well. Let stand until cool. Beat the egg whites until stiff peaks form; fold into the chocolate mixture. Pour into a buttered baking dish. Bake at 300 to 325 degrees for 20 minutes. Top each serving with a dollop of whipped cream.

Boiled Custard

Yield: 10 to 12 servings

3 to 4 cups milk

4 to 5 eggs

$1/2$ to 1 cup sugar

$1/4$ teaspoon salt

2 tablespoons flour

1 to 2 teaspoons vanilla extract

Brandy or bourbon to taste

Pour 1 cup of the milk over a mixture of the eggs, sugar, salt and flour in a mixer bowl; mix well. Scald the remaining milk in a saucepan. Stir a small amount of the scalded milk into the egg mixture; stir the egg mixture into the scalded milk in the saucepan. Cook until thickened and the mixture coats a spoon, stirring constantly. Stir in the vanilla. Pour into a mixer bowl. Beat for 1 to 2 minutes or until smooth. Pour into a serving container. Chill, covered, until serving time. Flavor with brandy or bourbon before serving. May strain the custard before serving. May omit brandy or bourbon.

But we're not going to change [the sign]. That's a trademark."
—Donna McCabe (*Milwaukee Journal* interview, Oct. 19, 1994)

Eggnog Killer Dessert

Yield: 10 servings

1 cup butter or margarine
1 (1-pound) package confectioners'
  sugar
6 egg yolks, beaten
1/2 cup whiskey
1 cup chopped black walnuts
6 egg whites, beaten
2/3 pound ladyfingers
1 pint whipping cream

Combine the butter and confectioners' sugar in a mixer bowl until light and fluffy. Add the egg yolks and whiskey gradually, mixing well after each addition. Stir in the walnuts. Fold in the egg whites. Split each ladyfinger. Line a buttered bowl with the ladyfingers halves. Alternate layers of the walnut mixture and ladyfingers until all ingredients are used, ending with the ladyfingers. Chill, covered, for 4 to 6 hours. Invert onto a serving plate. Whip the whipping cream. Spread the whipped cream over the top and side of the mound.

"We have a dessert that we serve at Christmas and Thanksgiving that we call Killebrew Killer Cake. What's the real name for it? Eggnog Cake. But we had a friend . . . who was from the north. So Thanksgiving I said, 'Why don't we invite him over . . . ?'

DESSERTS

Fruit Balls

Yield: 4 dozen

2 cups apricots

1 cup pecans

1/2 cup sugar

1 orange peel, grated

1/4 cup orange juice

1 cup confectioners' sugar

Process the apricots and pecans in a food processor until finely chopped. Combine the apricots, pecans, sugar, grated orange peel and orange juice in a bowl; mix well. Chill, covered, for 1 hour. Shape into balls. Roll in the confectioners' sugar.

Lemon Sponge Cake Dessert

Yield: 8 to 10 servings

2 tablespoons butter, softened

1 cup sugar

1/4 cup flour

Pinch of salt

5 tablespoons lemon juice

Rind of 1 lemon, grated

3 egg yolks, beaten

1 1/2 cups milk

3 egg whites, stiffly beaten

Whipped cream

Cream the butter in a large mixing bowl. Add the sugar, flour, salt, lemon juice and lemon rind. Stir in a mixture of the egg yolks and milk. Fold in the stiffly beaten egg whites. Pour the mixture into individual custard cups. Set the cups in a baking pan of water. Bake at 350 degrees for 45 minutes. Top each with a dollop of whipped cream.

Well, we served this eggnog cake, and he named it Killebrew Killer Cake. Soon as he ate all that turkey and dressing and cake . . . he stretched out on the couch and took a nap."

—Donna McCabe

Icebox Pineapple Dessert

Yield: 6 to 8 servings

1/2 cup melted butter

3 tablespoons cream

1 cup nuts

1 cup packed brown sugar

1 egg yolk, beaten

1 (8-ounce) can crushed pineapple

1 (12-ounce) package vanilla wafers, crushed

Combine the butter, cream, nuts, brown sugar, egg yolk and pineapple in a bowl; mix well. Alternate layers of the vanilla wafer crumbs and pineapple mixture in a serving dish until all ingredients are used. Chill, covered, for 4 to 6 hours before serving.

"Each serving of Lemon Sponge Cake Dessert will have custard in the bottom and sponge cake on the top."

Baked Pineapple Delight

Yield: 4 to 6 servings

1/2 cup margarine, softened

1/2 sugar

4 eggs

1 (15-ounce) can crushed pineapple, drained

8 slices bread, cut into cubes

Cream the margarine and sugar in a mixer bowl. Add the eggs 1 at a time, beating well after each addition. Stir in the pineapple and bread cubes. Spoon into a 1 1/2-quart baking dish. Bake at 325 degrees for 25 to 30 minutes.

Rum Sauce

Yield: 1 cup

1/4 cup sugar
4 teaspoons cornstarch
1/2 cup water
1/2 cup plus 1 teaspoon rum
2 tablespoons butter

Combine the sugar and cornstarch in a small saucepan. Stir in the water and rum. Cook over low heat until bubbly, stirring constantly. Remove from heat. Add the butter, stirring until the butter is melted.

Make-Ahead Sherry Dessert

Yield: 9 servings

1 (4-ounce) package vanilla instant
   pudding mix
1/2 cup milk
1/2 cup cream sherry
8 ounces whipped topping
1 small angel food cake

Combine the pudding mix and milk in a mixer bowl. Stir in the cream sherry. Fold in the whipped topping. Cut the cake into thin slices. Layer the slices over the bottom of an 8x8-inch dish. Spread the pudding mixture over the top. Chill, covered, for 8 hours or longer before serving.

"My husband enjoyed everything he put in his mouth, and it was fun to cook for him. So I loved to cook, especially for him."

—Mamie Strowd

DESSERTS

Whipped Cream Favorite

Yield: 8 servings

1 1/2 cups whipping cream
3/4 cup crushed pineapple
1/2 cup chopped cherries
3/4 cup chopped nuts
8 to 10 marshmallows, chopped
1 teaspoon vanilla extract
1/4 cup sugar

Whip the whipping cream in a mixer bowl. Fold in the pineapple, cherries, nuts and marshmallows. Add the vanilla and sugar; mix well. Spoon into a serving bowl. Chill, covered, until serving time.

"Once they get through eating, they go out with a smile. That's what it's all about."
—Donna McCabe

The Loveless Today

When her husband Charlie died in 1983, Donna McCabe faced a decision about what to do with the Loveless—but she didn't have to think more than a few seconds. "Of course I was going to keep it. It was ours. Besides, our younger son George wanted to get involved, and he has. We couldn't run it without George."

"We" these days includes Mamie Strowd, Donna's twin sister. Mamie runs the payroll and handles the mail-order business. Donna and Mamie are known in local lore by their maiden name—the Killebrew sisters.

After Charlie died, Donna added a new dimension to the Loveless— the mail-order business. "We always had people who wanted to order the jam or biscuits or ham," she says. "We couldn't keep up with the orders."

Part of the charm of the Loveless has been the characters who ran it, from Mr. Lon's booming storytelling voice to Stella Maynard's throwing the doors open to college fraternities. The Killebrew twins, with their friendly rivalry over their children and their habit of speaking the same thoughts in unison, fit right in.

Generations of the same families have not only eaten at the Loveless—they've also worked there. Mamie Greer waited tables from 1960 until 1984. Her daughter, Sherri Downing, started in 1976 and still works there. Sherri also has three children who've worked at the café at one time or another. Annie May Martin made the famous biscuits for more than 20 years.

It may be that the secret of the Loveless is in its very sameness. In a world that is rapidly changing, where today's highway becomes tomorrow's back road, this squat-looking old whitewashed roadside café is a blessed constant.

"It was always a good business," says Donna. "That part has never changed."

The Secret Recipe

Miss Annie Loveless created the recipe for the world-famous Loveless scratch biscuits during the 1950s after she and her husband bought the Harpeth Tea Room and turned it into the Loveless Motel and Café. When the Lovelesses sold the motel and restaurant to Stella and Cordell Maynard in 1960, the secret recipe was part of the transaction, and it was part of the transaction when the Maynards sold the Loveless to Donna and Charlie McCabe in 1974. No offered riches have induced the McCabes to part with the recipe.

Every person who has approached Donna McCabe with the idea that *he* or *she* will be the one who learns the secret recipe has been met with a pleasant refusal accompanied by a patient smile.

You'll have to come visit the Loveless Café if you want to taste those biscuits!

Substitutions

Cooking Tips

Instant Cooking Remedies

SUBSTITUTIONS

Baking Products

NEEDED INGREDIENT	SUBSTITUTION
1 teaspoon baking powder	$1/3$ teaspoon baking soda plus $1/2$ teaspoon cream of tartar
1 cup chopped pecans	1 cup regular oats, toasted
1 cup honey	$1^{1}/4$ cups sugar plus 1 cup water
1 cup light corn syrup	1 cup sugar plus $1/4$ cup water
1 (7-ounce) jar marshmallow cream	1 (16-ounce) package marshmallows, melted, plus $3^{1}/2$ tablespoons light corn syrup
1 cup powdered sugar	1 cup granulated sugar plus 1 tablespoon cornstarch (process in food processor)

Vegetable Products

NEEDED INGREDIENT	SUBSTITUTION
1 pound fresh mushrooms	1 (8-ounce) can sliced mushrooms, drained OR 3 ounces dried mushrooms
1 small onion, chopped	1 tablespoon instant minced onion
3 tablespoons chopped red or green pepper	1 tablespoon dried red or green pepper flakes
3 tablespoons chopped red pepper	2 tablespoons chopped pimentos
3 tablespoon chopped shallots	2 tablespoons chopped onion plus 1 tablespoon chopped garlic

SUBSTITUTIONS

Seasoning Products

NEEDED INGREDIENT	SUBSTITUTION
1 teaspoon ground allspice	$1/2$ teaspoon ground cinnamon plus $1/4$ teaspoon ground cloves
1 teaspoon apple pie spice	$1/2$ teaspoon ground cinnamon and $1/4$ teaspoon ground nutmeg
1 tablespoon chopped chives	1 tablespoon chopped green onion tops
1 clove garlic	$1/8$ teaspoon garlic powder or minced dried garlic
1 teaspoon garlic salt	$1/8$ teaspoon garlic powder plus $7/8$ teaspoon salt
1 tablespoon grated fresh gingerroot	$1/2$ teaspoon ground ginger
1 tablespoon candied ginger	$1/8$ teaspoon ground ginger
1 tablespoon grated fresh horseradish	2 tablespoons prepared horseradish
1 teaspoon dry mustard	1 tablespoon prepared mustard
1 tablespoon dried orange peel	$1 1/2$ teaspoons orange extract or 1 tablespoon grated orange rind
1 teaspoon pumpkin pie spice	$1/2$ teaspoon ground cinnamon, $1/4$ teaspoon ground ginger, and $1/8$ teaspoon ground allspice plus $1/8$ teaspoon ground nutmeg
1 (1-inch) vanilla bean	1 teaspoon vanilla extract plus $1/8$ teaspoon ground cinnamon

S U B S T I T U T I O N S

Dairy Products

NEEDED INGREDIENT	SUBSTITUTION
1 cup milk	1/2 cup evaporated milk plus 1/2 cup water
1 cup plain yogurt	1 cup buttermilk
1 cup sour cream	1 cup yogurt plus 3 tablespoons melted butter OR 1 cup yogurt plus 1 tablespoon cornstarch
1 cup whipping cream	3/4 cup milk plus 1/3 cup melted butter (for baking only; will not whip)

Miscellaneous Products

NEEDED INGREDIENT	SUBSTITUTION
1/2 cup balsamic vinegar	1/2 cup red wine vinegar
1 tablespoon brandy	1/4 teaspoon brandy extract plus 1 teaspoon water
1/4 cup marsala	1/4 cup dry white wine plus 1 teaspoon brandy
1 cup tomato juice	1/2 cup tomato sauce plus 1/2 cup water
2 cups tomato sauce	3/4 cups tomato paste plus 1 cup water

Substitute cottage cheese for ricotta. Cottage cheese yields a moist product; ricotta is "cheesier" in taste.

Sprinkle on a variety of cheeses. Experiment with Cheddar, American, Romano, Gouda, and Swiss. For a little spicy heat, try Monterey Jack with hot peppers.

Substitute spicy sausage when the recipe calls for ground beef. For a lower-fat dish, use the same amount of ground turkey or chicken.

Sample the new pre-cooked noodles available at the grocery store. Follow the directions on the package to eliminate the need to boil the noodles before baking.

COOKING TIPS

Vegetable Preparation Tips

• Steam vegetables over boiling water rather than in water. It preserves the vitamins.

• When cutting hot peppers, wear rubber gloves to keep the peppers from burning your hands.

• To prevent eggplant from darkening, do not cut it until ready to use. Lemon or lime juice on cut edges will help prevent darkening.

• Use leftover meats and vegetables in soups, stews, and salads.

Baking Tips

• It is no longer necessary to sift all-purpose or self-rising flour. Simply stir the flour, gently spoon it into a dry measuring cup, and level the top. Cake flour and powdered sugar, on the other hand, should be sifted to remove lumps.

• Regular and quick-cooking oats are essentially interchangeable, but regular oats add a chewy texture and are best when making granola, cookies, desserts, and pie crust.

• Preheat the oven 10 minutes before baking.

• Do not open the oven door while cooking as the temperature drops 20 to 30 degrees when the door is opened. The oven window can be used to save energy.

• Be sure that the expiration date on yeast has not passed. Be sure to dissolve yeast in water that is between 105 and 115 degrees Fahrenheit. Hot water can kill the yeast and prevent baked goods from rising. Cold water slows down the process.

INSTANT COOKING REMEDIES

Problem
Stewed fruit is turning sour.

Solution
Add a pinch of baking soda to the fruit; reboil for 5 minutes.

Problem
Too much sugar is needed to sweeten very sour fruit.

Solution
Add a pinch of salt to stewing fruit.

Problem
Hands smell from onions or garlic.

Solution
Rinse hands in cold water; rub with salt or baking soda; rinse again; wash with soap and water.

Problem
Cooking onions or cabbage create a strong odor.

Solution
Boil 1 cup of vinegar on the stovetop.

Problem
Rice is sticky.

Solution
Rinse rice thoroughly with warm water to wash out the excess starch; grains will separate.

INSTANT COOKING REMEDIES

Problem
Eggshell cracks while egg is boiling.

Solution
Add a few drops of vinegar to the water; use eggs at room temperature.

Problem
One egg short for a recipe.

Solution
Substitute 1 teaspoon cornstarch.

Problem
Omelet is tough and rubbery.

Solution
Add 1 scant teaspoon boiling water per egg to mixture.

Problem
Bread is slightly stale.

Solution
Sprinkle bread with water or milk; wrap in aluminum foil; bake at 350 degrees for about 8 minutes. If bread is hard crusted, open the foil and bake for 3 to 5 minutes more.

Problem
Coffee cake is dry.

Solution
Put 2 tablespoons water or milk in a large skillet; place un-iced cake on trivet in skillet. Cover; leave over low heat for about 8 minutes. When freshening iced cake, do not cover.

INSTANT COOKING REMEDIES

Problem
Keep sugar soft and moist.
Solution
Place a slice of bread or a couple of saltine crackers in sugar container; cover tightly.

Problem
Brown sugar is caked and hard.
Solution
Place brown sugar in a 200-degree oven until it is dry and crumbly; powder it in an electric blender or with a mortar and pestle.

Problem
Added too much sugar to something.
Solution
Add a few drops of lemon juice or vinegar.

Problem
Added too much salt to something.
Solution
Add a little vinegar; taste. A raw potato in soups or stews helps to absorb salt.

Problem
Fish has a strong odor.
Solution
Rub fish with lemon juice and salt to prevent the odor from being absorbed by other food.

INSTANT COOKING REMEDIES

Problem
Leftover cheese is dried out.

Solution
Store cheese (unprocessed) in freezer; once frozen, it will crumble easily. Slice thin without thawing to use in recipes that call for grated cheese.

Problem
Cheese is coated with mold.

Solution
Cheese flavor will not be affected. Wipe mold off with paper towels soaked in vinegar; scrap heavy mold off with a knife. Recover loosely with plastic wrap.

Problem
Frying oil has a strong odor.

Solution
After frying strong-flavored foods, cool oil; clarify it by adding a raw potato, then reheating slowly. Discard potato; strain and store oil.

Problem
Sauce or gravy is lumpy.

Solution
Pour sauce or gravy through a strainer and mash out the lumps with a wooden spoon. Reheat very slowly.

Problem
Brewed tea is weak.

Solution
Add a pinch of baking soda to the teapot.

INSTANT COOKING REMEDIES

Problem

Coffee tastes bitter.

Solution

Put a pinch of salt into coffee that has brewed too long.

Problem

Brewed coffee is weak.

Solution

Add a little instant coffee to the pot; this will strengthen it without changing the taste.

Problem

Mayonnaise is curdled or separated.

Solution

In a warmed bowl, beat 1 tablespoon curdled mayonnaise with whisk until creamy. Add mayonnaise slowly until blended.

Problem

Gravy has too much fat.

Solution

Cool the liquid; skim the fat off the top or pour liquid through ice cubes into a bowl. The fat will solidify and can be removed easily.

Problem

Cake has cracked in the middle.

Solution

The oven was too hot or the temperature was uneven during baking. Disguise crack with icing.

INSTANT COOKING REMEDIES

Problem

Cake rises too much, overflows pan.

Solution

Batter had too much baking powder, too little flour, or the pan was filled more than 2/3 full.

Problem

Cake rises in oven, caves in when cooling.

Solution

Pan was overfilled, or egg whites were beaten when recipe didn't call for it. Fill in with frosting.

Problem

Cake has shiny slick streak.

Solution

This is caused by poor mixing, too-slow baking, or irregular heating of pan in oven.

Problem

Cake is sticky.

Solution

Too much liquid or too much sugar was used, or baking powder was too old.

INDEX

INDEX

INDEX

INDEX

INDEX

INDEX

A Box Full of Recipes

It began with a little brown box stuffed full of recipes that had been handed down from mother to daughter and cherished by family members for many years. Donna and Mamie collaborated in selecting the best from their treasured family collection. Each had tried working at home on the project, but that didn't work very well for either, so they worked together in the back of the trailer behind the café.

"She sits at one desk and I sit at another one and every now and then we'll speak to each other," said Mamie when she and her sister were halfway through the job of carefully sorting, selecting, and testing recipes.

Some of the recipes were acquired from friends as well as from family members. Many had never been written down before, but had existed until now only in the heads and the experiences of the twins. It was sometimes a struggle for Mamie, the "natural cook" of the two, to assign quantities and measured time periods to an activity that for her had always been a matter of instinct and artistry. Both were pleased with the collection that came out of their labors.

Use the lines on the next page to keep track of your own favorite recipes from this incredible family collection.

FAVORITES

Recipe Title	Page No.

There are many ways to get to the Loveless Café . . .

From Downtown Nashville:
Broadway (70S) to West End Ave. (70S) to Harding Rd. (70S) to Hwy 100 & 70S fork. Bear left at fork to Hwy. 100. 7^1/$_2$ miles on right.

From I-65 Louisville:
I-65 South to I-265 South to I-40 West. See directions for I-40 Knoxville.

From I-65 Birmingham:
I-65 North to I-40 West. See directions for I-40 Knoxville.

From I-24 St. Louis:
I-24 East to I-65 South to I-265 South to I-40 West. See directions for I-40 Knoxville.

From I-24 Chattanooga:
I-24 West to I-40 West. See directions for I-40 Knoxville.

From I-40 Memphis:
I-40 East to Exit 192, McCrory Lane. Turn right. 4 miles to Hwy. 100, turn left. 100 yards on left. (Large vehicles and in bad weather, take Exit 199, Old Hickory Blvd. Turn right. 3.8 miles to Hwy. 100, turn right. 3.8 miles on right.)

From I-40 Knoxville:
I-40 West to Exit 199, Old Hickory Blvd. Turn left. 3.8 miles to Hwy. 100, turn right. 3.8 miles on right.

VISIT THE LOVELESS

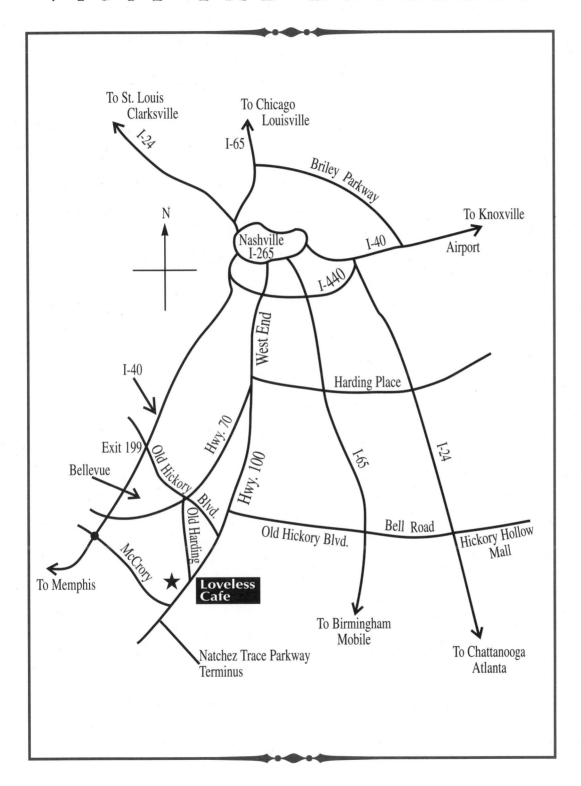